E
18/7

Praise for *The Essential Digital Interview Handbook*

"Readers with an entrepreneurial mindset will devour *The Essential Digital Interview Handbook* because it provides the road map to successful sales and marketing engagement over the web."

—Ilya Pozin, CEO of Open Me, columnist for *Inc*, *Forbes*, and LinkedIn, serial entrepreneur

"This is the best time to learn everything you can about digital interviewing techniques, and Paul Bailo's well-researched knowledge will keep you ahead of the curve."

—Christine Giordano, *Newsday* journalist and writer/producer, *On Your Watch*

"Paul Bailo's *The Essential Digital Interview Handbook* is a great service—practical, well written, data driven insights and wisdom. Reading this book will allow you to perform as a senior executive in the digital world. A wonderful creation."

—Peter Horn, chairman at Euro-Capital Group, Inc.

"It's just as important for executive recruiters, like me, to project a professional image in virtual interviews with my clients and applicants. That's why I read *The Essential Digital Interview Handbook*."

—Ralph F. Conserva, president of Conserva Resources, Inc.
25+ years of Executive Placement

"Luck is another word for opportunity and with the guidance of *The Essential Digital Interview Handbook*, you will jumpstart your job search and magnify your chances for stellar face-to-face performances via technology for any interview."

—Cynthia Brian, *New York Times* best-selling author, radio personality, and founder/executive director, Be the Star You Are!® 501 c3 literacy charity

THE ESSENTIAL
Digital
Interview
HANDBOOK

LIGHTS, CAMERA, INTERVIEW:
TIPS FOR SKYPE,
GOOGLE HANGOUT,
GOTOMEETING,
AND MORE

PAUL J. BAILO

CAREER
PRESS
Pompton Plains, NJ

THE ESSENTIAL DIGITAL INTERVIEW HANDBOOK
EDITED BY KIRSTEN DALLEY
TYPESET BY EILEEN MUNSON
Cover design by Jeff Piasky
Printed in the U.S.A.

To order this title, please call toll-free 1-800-CAREER-1 (NJ and Canada: 201-848-0310) to order using VISA or MasterCard, or for further information on books from Career Press.

The Career Press, Inc.
220 West Parkway, Unit 12
Pompton Plains, NJ 07444
www.careerpress.com

Library of Congress Cataloging-in-Publication Data
CIP Data Available Upon Request

To my family:
Kathleen, Connor, and
Kaitlyn.
And our new puppy,
Fenway.

ACKNOWLEDGMENTS

There's no question that this book would never have happened if it weren't for the constant support of my family and friends. I want to thank my wife, Kathleen, and our wonderful children, Connor and Kaitlyn, who allowed me to miss baseball games, soccer games, and quality family time while Daddy wrote a book to help others. Thank you to the rest of my family and friends who keep me energized, excited, and moving forward.

To the team at Career Press, thank you. To Adam Schwartz, my acquisitions editor, thank you for bringing life to my book. A special thank-you to Kirsten Dalley, whose wisdom and creative editing added significant value to the book. I could not have done it without you.

And to Gareth Esersky at the Carol Mann Agency, thank you for taking my call, meeting me at the bookstore, and making the book deal happen. Next stop: world book tour!

Finally, a big thank you must go to Amanda Stoll. Amanda helped to organize and edit all the material on my previous book, *The Essential Phone Interview Handbook*, and, after much success on that project, has come back to assist with my second book. Her experience using Skype to conduct her own job search from Bangkok has made her a key player in assembling and refining the content. Her detail-oriented nature and her intelligent sense of humor brought grammatical structure and witty examples to this book, making it one that can be easily understood and applied to virtually all readers. Thank you, Amanda, for all your hard work.

Contents

PART THREE: CONCLUDING

FOREWORD

People say that 50 percent of getting any job is getting the chance to sit across the desk from the hiring manager. Seems right to me, but over the years, it has also been my experience that in their desire to get there, lots of candidates are so focused on that objective that they forget about the first 50 percent, or at least they take a lot of it for granted.

People think that the name of the game, especially in these cyber times, is to get a resume and then fire salvo after salvo into the ether and wait for a phone call, e-mail, or text message—an oversimplification perhaps, but sad to say, not all that far off.

To say that the competition for opportunities in today's marketplace is intense would be an understatement. What many of us don't think about when we find ourselves involved in this competition is that the first 50 percent is even tougher than the second 50 percent. After all, think of how many competitors get screened digitally or otherwise before they become one of the four to six finalists who actually get to sit across the aforementioned desk. Your percentages are a lot better when you are in the face-to-face stage than if you are one of the 200, plus or minus, who are actually contacted out of the thousands who apply.

There is also a saying that the definition of luck is when preparation meets opportunity. Whether it is Skype, Google Hangout, Facebook, video conferences, or Google glasses, the degree to which you understand and master how to present yourself effectively in today's digital world will determine your ability to make it from the first 50 percent to the second.

This book will help you make your own "luck."

Dave Opton, Founder, ExecuNet

E-mail: dopton@execunet.com

Website: *www.execunet.com*

PREFACE

Whatever possessed me to write a book about digital communication, specifically in the area of digital job interviewing? Well, the truth of the matter is, I love research, I love data, and I love helping people to succeed. The key component of my desire to write this book is to help people be successful. Based on my research, my numerous personal interviews, and discussion with industry leaders, I have developed the ability to get to the core components of what you need to be successful in your digital job interviews.

I have been thinking about digital job interviewing for quite some time, telling my publisher, agent, family, and friends that there is a huge market and need for a book on the subject. Communicating via the Web is growing exponentially, but based on my research, we are all doing a terrible job at it. We think we can just turn on the computer, power up our Webcams, and turn up the volume and we are good to go. That is not how it works in the professional world. We can't blame society for this, because until now, no one has been educated on how to conduct or give a digital job interview. No one has done the research and used a methodical combination of surveys, data collection, and analysis to determine how this form of communication really works. No one has come to a solid, educated conclusion based on real information—until now. This book, which has essentially been in my head for the past year, is at your disposal to help you master this new and exciting skill.

I have had the good fortune to present at numerous national, international, and world-class organizations sharing my insights on my first book, *The Essential Phone Interview Handbook*. At every lecture, there is always a question about digital job interviewing. From lectures at Ivy League universities to CEOs in transition, they all want to know: How do you conduct a digital job interview? I've received numerous questions from recruiters and executive colleagues on how one can shine in a world-class digital videoconference. This got me thinking that there is clearly a need to help people perfect their digital interviewing skills. I spoke with numerous executives in the recruiting industry while conducting my research in order to help you get the most out of your digital job interviews. There is a methodical approach to being successful in this medium, and this book will teach you how to master it. You will learn how to be professional, energetic, memorable, engaging, and real. There is no greater goal in life than helping others, and so, in this way, I consider your success my success. Help me help you perform to your utmost in your next digital job interview.

The fun part about writing this book was that there was no other book like it in the marketplace. This is a completely untouched niche, one that is advancing so quickly that no one has taken the time to help people perform at the new high-class level. Until now.

What This Book Is Not

This book is not a highly technical digital manual on software, technology, or equipment. It is not an all-consumer report from Best Buy for a selection of video conferencing software, microphones, or cameras. Even though I will give you my opinion on what has worked well in the lab when I was writing this book, it is not a book that rates, grades, or selects specific products or companies to promote. It is, however, a book that should be read by people who want to improve their digital presence in the video interview and conferencing arena. The tools you use, the software and equipment you select, should be based on your own research.

How to Use This Book

You probably think this is a pretty silly thing to discuss—of course you know how to use a book! You find a nice, cozy spot at home and you start reading. Pretty straightforward. However, reading this book is slightly different. Before you even open it, you want to be in the right mindset; you also need to get clear on your expectations regarding what you wish to gain from reading it. Also, you must try to remain open-minded. A number of the key points you may not like, but remember, this is based on hard data. What I am asking of you is precisely what the marketplace will be demanding from you if you want to perform at an extremely high level on your digital interviews. If you are not looking to perform on a world-class stage, this is not the book for you.

Perhaps most importantly, you need to determine what aspects of digital job interviewing work for you and which ones you think you might need help or assistance with. Create a simple formula that fits your situation that will lead you to success. Determine what chapters will help you the most and leave the rest for another time. Ultimately my goal is to help you, whether that means you read the whole book or just parts of it.

Who Will Benefit From This Book?

The beneficiaries of this book are obvious: job candidates, recruiters, executives, educational professionals, professors, teachers of all kinds, people with special needs, members of international book clubs, anyone in the field of professional development, company customer service departments that engage digital media to help them drive high-level customer service, anyone looking for help with homework, participants in town hall meetings, marketing executives, judges, lawyers, doctors, and the list goes on. If you are looking to upgrade your skills and embrace digital technology, there's no question that this book will be of value to you.

Introduction:

What Is a Digital Interview?

Think of a digital interview as your own personal Flat Stanley. Don't know what a Flat Stanley is? *Flat Stanley* is a children's book written by Jeff Brown. In the book, a bulletin board falls on the young boy named Stanley when he is sleeping and flattens him. He takes advantage of this interesting condition by sliding under doors and even getting himself mailed to different friends in an envelope. This book has become a popular grade-school classroom project, wherein kids create their own "Flat Stanleys" and mail them to friends and family members all around the world. In a digital job interview, *you* are a Flat Stanley. You're a flat, two-dimensional image being projected through your computer, over the Web, and right onto the interviewer's monitor.

Videoconferencing has become increasingly popular in today's world as technology advances ever more rapidly. More and more people are using the Internet to conduct meetings, give interviews, and engage in discussions. This simple process eliminates travel time and is far more personable than "meeting" someone over the phone. My research indicates that the digital job interview is fast on the rise, so you need to be ready to perform at a competitive level.

It all starts with an opening you find interesting. You start networking and, hopefully, get the opportunity to have a phone interview. If all goes well, you are scheduled for a digital interview. As you can see, with each step, a new dimension is added:

▷ The phone interview is one-dimensional—sound.

▷ The digital job interview is two-dimensional—sound and sight.

▷ The face-to-face interview is three-dimensional—sound, sight, and feel.

The ultimate goal is to make your digital job interviews as real as possible, which means you must be able to connect through this digital medium.

Communicating through this medium is foreign to many people. The problem is that they believe their mock broadcast studio does not have to change to emphasize the overall feeling they are trying to get across to the other person. On the contrary, everything must vary to communicate human emotion and professionalism through this mere two-dimensional medium. This is why I have written this book—not only for important job interviews, but also for everyday communication on the Web. Regardless of the software, equipment, or scenario, this book will be invaluable to you.

You might be wondering why an organization that was looking to hire someone wouldn't just call you in for a meeting rather than putting you (and them) through this initial digital screening. Well, a lot of it has to do with cost and time efficiency. It is much cheaper to interview candidates over the Internet than to fly them in, buy them lunch, and put them up in a hotel. It is also more time efficient, as interviewees don't have to dedicate their precious time to travel. With a job market that is becoming more global by the day, it is easier for all parties to initiate this digital interview phase. The good thing is that you, the candidate, also have the opportunity to evaluate the hiring manager and get a better feel for him or her than you would over the phone. (Remember, first you speak with them over the phone, and then, if all goes well, you proceed to the the digital job interview.)

This concept of interviewing over the Web is relatively new but it's here to stay. The digital interview is becoming more popular among hiring companies as the applicant pool expands to an international level. Want to move across the country but need a job first? Are you volunteering in a foreign country but looking for a job closer to home? Studying abroad and trying to secure a position for after graduation? The digital interview is the next step in making a connection between interviewer and interviewee without their having to be in the same room. As this field advances, technology and human competitiveness will also advance, so it is essential that you start now—first by reading this book—to be successful in this medium.

Digital job interviews are the closest thing we have to face-to-face interviews. Therefore, interacting over the Web in this context needs to be as close to an actual physical interaction as possible. Obviously there is no replacement for the human element of being able to shake someone's hand and look the person in the eye to get a good sense of his or her character, the fullness of who this person is, and what he/she stands for. However, digital interviewing can get you to a pretty close approximation of this. The next best thing to getting to know someone in person is by using a Webcam and a strong Internet connection. For the hiring party, this is an easy way to filter out job candidates without spending excessive money or time. For the candidate, it's a great way to get a sense of who you might be working for. Digital interviewing is here to stay, so it is important to start learning now about how to be a top competitor and maximize this new channel of communication.

This book is not just about digital interviews. It applies to anyone who uses a Webcam to communicate with others. Whether you are talking with your relatives in Europe or conducting a multiple person conference from different office locations by using Skype, Facebook, or Videochat, you can benefit from this book. I no longer want to see people in their offices talking to colleagues in different parts of the world with their heads chopped off, the image pixilated, and the sound delayed. I don't want to see job candidates with shadows on their faces as they try to get a job. I don't want to see anyone spend three months doing their research and then not get the position because they look terrible on the hiring manager's screen (because they don't know how to position the camera or set up their lighting or background, for example). I don't want otherwise intelligent and qualified students who are seeking internships to be at a disadvantage because they just turn on their laptop and start talking during their digital job interviews. I don't want to see candidates do tons of research on the company and the hiring manager, but zero research on the technical aspects of the interview itself. This kind of thing happens every day, but all these mistakes and more can be fixed by educating yourself.

When you are preparing for and conducting your digital job interview, you must realize that *you* are the star. Think of yourself as a Hollywood star with your own studio. And you're not only the star; you're also the director, producer, writer, set designer, make-up artist, costume designer, and cameraperson. Every responsibility that goes into a broadcast is yours. You have to wrap up all these positions into one with the ultimate goal of communicating who you are and what you do via your computer. This is what it takes to communicate and advance over the Web.

In this two-dimensional format, sight and sound have enormous power, especially if you are talking to multiple people simultaneously. The way you harness this power is both an art and a science. You really have to put your entire heart, soul, and mind into communicating over that digital line. You want to be able to reach out and figuratively touch the person on the other end of your conversation, even though you're essentially a Flat Stanley. You may be flat on the screen, but you must establish a relationship that is whole and multidimensional.

What Is Skype?

Some hiring managers use an application called Skype. Skype is an Internet application that allows for any person to conduct video and voice calls to any other Skype account in the world. It is easy to download and free to use. Skype enables you to have a conversation with one person or a group of people in another country or hemisphere. Don't know how to use Skype? This book will teach you. By using Skype, applicants can take the next step in building their career.

PART ONE:

PREPARING

1. SOFTWARE

The heart of your operation for your personalized digital interviewing studio lies in the software. However, this book is not software specific. Whether you are using Google Hangout or Skype or GoToMeeting or any other video chatting software, all I ask is that you are comfortable with it. But you must be proficient enough to leverage the power of whatever software product you choose.

In my own, personal videoconference studio, I favor Google Hangout because it is simple and powerful. It makes life easy when connecting with another person for a digital job interview. You just have to make sure you have all the right components and it runs on the right frequency in terms of what product software the other person is using. You also cannot go wrong with using Skype, a major player in the videoconferencing world now owned by Microsoft. A third option, which I have nothing bad to say about, is GoToMeeting, another product that is easy to use.

This book is not an endorsement of one product over another. It is encouraging the use of any of these products to assist you in performing at the highest level. As time goes on, greater and greater advancements in video chatting are taking place, so there will always be a newer software system to use. This book will be able to support you and propel you forward no matter which software or technology product you choose to use.

The core component is not just the software, but how you control the software in combination with the lighting, sound, background, and script. The combination of how you put it all together to create the success story of you communicating, connecting and leveraging the digital job interviewing process is of utmost importance. You must use your software to create a powerful, emotional connection with the person on the other end.

Story With a Moral

I remember Sam, a senior in college, telling me how great all the new video software packages were with their new amazing features. However, Sam seemed unable to use this software to get past the digital interview and land a face-to-face meeting. He had digital interviews with several big-name companies, but they never led to an in-person meeting. He was an expert on the software—in fact, he could even write the code for Skype—yet he could not perform well on camera. Why? He forgot that the show was about him, not the equipment he used. Software is simply a tool, just as a paintbrush is a tool for an artist. You can paint a magnificent landscape with lush colors on a canvas, or you can create a game of tick-tack-toe on a piece of paper. The difference in the outcome is the artist, not the paintbrush.

Moral of the Story	*The tools of the trade are all great products, but the focus is* **you**. *Leverage the tools to help you land the job.*

2. Camera

The essential part of the digital job interview is the camera. Now, choosing a camera can be a bit overwhelming, as there are hundreds if not thousands of different makes and models of Webcams out there. Let me help you narrow the selection. After extensive research, the camera that stands out the most is a Logitech HD Pro Webcam C920. As of this writing, it costs about 100 dollars. This camera is easy to use, has a high pixel count, and, as I found while conducting our tests in digital interviewing, it creates a clear, vibrant picture. I have no relationship with Logitech, Hewlett-Packard, or any other manufacturer of Webcams. There are numerous cameras that will get the job done. But if you're looking for the best, the Logitech rose to the top of our selection process as a simple, easy-to-use Webcam that gives the best quality picture for the price.

Along with the camera, you must also purchase a tripod. Dangling your camera on the edge of your computer monitor is a definite no-no. You cannot get the correct angle or the optimal lighting with the camera in this position. You also want to be able to have a direct line of sight between your eyes and the camera so you can look at the other person as if they were actually sitting in front of you. This can only be done with a tripod. If possible, get a tripod that was made for the camera. If there isn't one, you can use a generic model. You want to make sure your camera is sitting in front of your monitor screen at eye level while conducting your digital job interview.

I do not recommend using a built-in laptop camera due to the professional image that is required in this competitive market. It is too difficult to get the correct angle when you cannot move your camera independently of your computer. I also would not recommend using a smartphone. I know the latest versions take amazing pictures, but it this not the optimal way to conduct a professional videoconference. Getting a high-definition Webcam on a tripod in front of your monitor is the best, and really the only, way to go.

You can search the Internet for different Webcam ratings to find what camera you'll be most comfortable with. The product you choose has to feel right for you, and you have to make sure it makes you look great. If you are not comfortable with it, you won't look good during your videoconference, and we don't want that.

Another aspect to consider is that you must make sure all the parts fit together. The camera must be on the same performance level as your Internet provider. If you buy a high-quality HD Webcam, but you have poor Internet service, then you are going to have quite a challenge making everything connect smoothly. You have to check that you have the bandwidth to support the camera you are purchasing for your digital interview. If your Internet service provider cannot deliver your image in the high-resolution brilliance of your Webcam, then your connection will be negatively affected. You do not want to look like you are in slow motion because your technology is not in sync!

It always amazes me when I am on vacation and I see people traveling to these glorious places around the world with a cheap camera that doesn't yield high-quality photographs. Of course, that is their personal life and their decision. However, this is your professional life. You need to spend the money on an HD Webcam with the tripod; it's that simple. This is what the marketplace demands, and I guarantee you will not regret it when you experience the image quality during your digital interview.

If you don't have the funds available to get an HD camera and you have to use the camera built into your laptop (which, again, I do not recommend), you should at least try to raise your laptop so it is at eye level. I don't mean you should hold up your laptop the entire time; rather, find a sturdy support, like a small shelf, to put it on so you can look directly at the camera. Remember, straight on at eye level is where you want to be.

If you plan on disregarding my advice and use your smartphone to conduct your digital job interviews, you should at least purchase a stand for it. That way, at least you'll have the tripod part of the equipment. Be aware this camera is not the best quality, but it will do the job if necessary.

Remember, the optimal way to get the desired professional image is to purchase a name-brand HD Webcam and position it on a tripod sitting in front of your screen at eye level so you can look right at the camera as you are conducting your interviews.

S tory With a Moral

I remember conducting a digital interview for a senior-level marketing position at a Fortune 500 company. The candidate came highly recommended, so I thought this would be an easy interview. It wasn't. The camera the candidate was using was of very poor quality, and he appeared fuzzy and hazy—it was almost as though I was looking thorough a kaleidoscope on my computer screen.

Moral of the Story	*Don't turn your image into a kaleidoscope of fuzzy, hazy colors on the interviewer's computer screen. Invest in a high-quality, name-brand Webcam and show your true colors during your digital interviews.*

3. Audio

"Can you hear me now? Testing, testing, one-two-three." This is exactly what you do *not* want to happen during your digital job interviews, or during any other meeting or conference you hold over the Web. It will make you look unprofessional and unprepared. To put it simply, this cannot happen.

The funny (but also not-so-funny) part is that during my research for this stage of the book, it was mind-boggling to me how hard it is for people to hear each other over the Web. One of the main problems is the lack of high-quality audio equipment. Basically, you are what you sound like. If you sound as though you have marbles in your mouth due to inferior audio equipment, this is going to reflect badly on you. You need to upgrade your audio equipment from the standard computer audio to a Webcam microphone. You are going to have to spend some money, not a lot of money, but at least $100 dollars on audio for your digital interview. Remember, this is for you to sound extremely clear and professional. If you invest you will have little to no misunderstandings caused by audio during your digital job interview. It's that simple.

So now that you have gotten over the fact that you have to spend $100 dollars on equipment, let me tell you what you are going to need. I use a microphone from a company called Blue. They make an outstanding product specifically for interviewing called the Snowball. The exact microphone you want to order is a Blue Snowball USB microphone. It was the best microphone that we tested in the lab, and I use it personally. Be aware that this microphone does have a vintage look to it (it reminds me of something you would see from the early days of radio). But don't be fooled into thinking that because it looks old, it must not be top quality. With the Blue snowball microphone, you will also need a shock mount, which holds the microphone in place to eliminate any unnecessary vibrations and unwanted sounds created by any movement.

Finally, you'll need a six-inch pop filter. This will remove all that annoying popping sound that you sometimes get with microphones. It basically resembles a screen that hooks directly to the microphone stand. Then you will have the utmost sound quality for your digital interviews.

In summary, here are the top three items that my research indicates are among the best audio pieces for your digital interview:

1. Blue Snowball microphone.
2. Ringer with universal shock mount for the b microphone.
3. Pop filter—6 inch MPF 6.
4. Stand.

When I purchased my equipment on Amazon.com it came out to about $99 dollars. This is an incredible deal for the quality of sound you'll experience during your videoconferences. If you look great, but you don't sound great, you're missing half of the story. When I think of people who have poor audio equipment for conducting digital job interviews, I think of them as actors in a Charlie Chaplin movie. If you are a Charlie Chaplin fan, you'll know that he was a great actor and producer of silent movies. This works for the film industry, but not for the digital interviewing industry. Don't be Charlie Chaplin. Go out and spend the money on high-quality equipment. Once again, the Blue Snowball microphone is the one I have in my own office. When people stop by my office most ask, "What the heck is that thing?" Most people are unfamiliar with the Blue microphones. They're not aware that this vintage-looking microphone is actually fantastic in terms of its sound quality. You can search the Internet yourself to see which microphone you like best, but I have done the homework, and this is the one you want. You will sound extremely professional. You can have the microphone positioned where it belongs, outside the camera range for your digital interview, and it works perfectly.

If you want to find your own microphone, by all means, do so. However, I do not recommend clip-on microphones (also called lavaliers). This is distracting during a digital interview and, frankly, it's also a bit showy—you are not a secret agent conducting a mission; you are a professional job candidate. So stay away from clip-on microphones and headsets during your interviews. Don't let your microphone distract from what you are trying to accomplish, which is to connect, communicate, and, ultimately, get the job. Even if you are not on an interview, keep your microphone out of sight and out of mind.

Have you ever walked around your favorite city and seen a movie or TV show being filmed? You've probably noticed the camera and sound people running around with those gigantic, fuzzy microphones. This is certainly not what you need for your digital job interviews. Bigger does not mean better. Every microphone is designed for a specific purpose and setting. You need your microphone to be positioned relatively close to the camera so you are looking at the camera and projecting your voice. I like to set up my microphone right underneath my camera; that way, I can still look the other person in the eyes when I'm speaking, and he/she has no clue that there is this slightly goofy-looking microphone right in front of me. I sound great and look great, and everything is clicking because I did my research and made the purchases necessary to complete the package.

I'm not saying you can't use the microphone on your Logitech camera or the one that's built into your laptop. I am trying to get you to the highest level of performance. As my father always says, it takes money to make money. In order to be successful on a digital job interview and to actually get the job, you have to sound good, and you have to spend a few dollars to get there. I know you can buy a camera that includes audio, but I prefer to separate the sight and sound components of the digital job interview. This way, you get the best product for each aspect. Buy a camera that is solely focused on making you look good. Buy a microphone that is solely focused on making you sound good. Then, put them together and you have an amazing digital interview performance. If you do choose to go on the path of the combined camera with microphone, just be aware that the quality may not be as good.

Story With a Moral

It always amazes me when a candidate uses an inferior-quality microphone that is almost guaranteed to detract from his or her professional image during interviews. I remember conducting a digital interview for a senior technology role; all was going great until the candidate opened her mouth. She sounded like Alvin from *Alvin and the Chipmunks*. She had a high-pitched, piercing voice that resonated through your ears when she spoke. Did she really have a voice like Alvin? Not at all. She was using a poor-quality audio system that turned her voice into a cartoon character. Definitely not the impression you want to convey during your digital interviews!

Moral of the Story

Spend the money and get a high-quality audio system for your digital interviews so the hiring managers don't mistake you for a well-known cartoon character.

4. LIGHTING STUDIO

Let there be light! Without decent light, how can you conduct a digital job interview (or any interview, for that matter)? Lighting can make or break your digital job interview, so let's get it right the first time. It is simply a matter of flipping the right switch.

Of the many elements that make a great movie, lighting is one of the most important. In my research, in talking to the executives working in our trials, lighting turns out to be one of the most critical components to a digital job interview. Not just lighting, but the right lighting is paramount to successful digital job interviews. And not just the right lighting, but the right lighting at the right angle is key. You cannot have lighting that is distracting; you need lighting that focuses on and illuminates the subject. How do you get the best lighting? The best lighting comes from practice and experience. You have to understand that lighting is an extremely powerful tool. It sets the mood by controlling the atmosphere that the viewers perceive. You do not want to be in a position where lighting is hurting the probability of you getting hired or connecting with the person interviewing you. I want to make sure you fully understand how important it is to your success that you master this component of the digital interview.

What kind of lighting do you need? Well, the one kind you *don't* need is overhead lighting. This creates undesirable shadows on your face. You need front and back lighting to create a clear, professional image of yourself. For this, you are going to need three sources of light. The first light will be to the right of you at a 30-degree angle; the second light will be to your left at a 20-degree angle; and the third light will be behind you, pointing forward. The goal is to have soft, natural lighting that eliminates all shadows and frames your profile. Of course, we are not all multimillionaires capable of building a high-tech studio, so let me teach you how I did it, the average-Queens-New-York-guy-kind-of-way.

First, the light bulbs. You need to get CFL natural soft lighting. Not hard or brilliant sunlight lighting, but nice, gentle lighting coming from those three sources. After you have your light bulbs, go to Home Depot and get some clothes pins—you know, those things your grandmother used to use to hang clothing out to dry. You'll also need some spring clips, extension cords, diffusion paper, and some inexpensive light stands. In addition, purchase three scoop-shaped lamps for lighting. The lights need to be just above your eye line. You may also want to invest in a surge protector just in case there is a power surge during your digital job interview. Now that you have all these things, here's how to set up the optimal lighting for your digital job interview, Webinar, or videoconference.

Place two of the lights right behind your Webcam—one to the right and one to the left of the camera. Make sure the light is not being projected into the camera, but is being used to illuminate your entire face. (Remember, shadows during a digital job interview are a definite no-no.) The lights should be about three feet away from your camera, depending on your home studio setup. You will have to play with it and test it out to make sure the lights are at the proper distance.

Now, using the clothes pins you bought, affix the diffusion paper over the scoop-shaped shades. This will create the soft lighting you want, extinguishing shadows and creating a flattering glow.

The third light should go directly behind you, lighting up the background. You now have a triangular format for your lighting—right, left, and back. This is the perfect way to set up the lighting for your digital job interview. Be aware that having three lights shining on you for an hour can make you feel a bit warm. Make sure you can control the room temperature. If your interview is taking place in the winter, turn down your heat; if it is the summer; turn up the air conditioning (just make sure that the window unit or air vents do not distract from the audio). You need the temperature in the room to be on the cool side so that you don't sweat your way through your interviews. You don't want to look like a nervous broadcaster constantly wiping sweat from your brow.

What this chapter really comes down to is a simple formula to create soft, natural light with three well-positioned light stands and some diffusion paper. If you do it correctly, you will have a natural ambience that eliminates any shadows. Every studio is different, so feel free to add another light or slightly modify their locations if need be. Of course, if you have the money, you can go to Home Depot and purchase a home lighting kit with a variety of lighting accessories for around $300 dollars. But, if you are willing to get bit crafty, you can save some money and create the same lighting impact the average-Queens-New-York-guy-kind-of-way. Whichever way you choose, set up your lights in the right direction and at the right angle to create the professional environment designed for success.

Story With a Moral

I remember conducting an executive conference with my executive team for people in New York, Connecticut, Hong Kong, and London. The gentleman from London hopped on his computer, turned on his office lights, and expected to be viewed in a professional manner. The light he switched on was a fluorescent light in the center of his office, so throughout this global conference call, he looked like a sideways Phantom of the Opera. The top of his bald head had the light projecting off of it, but from his nose down there was a big shadow. What would have helped was some front and back lighting, as I've described here, but instead there was a video image that did not portray this otherwise qualified executive in the best light.

Moral of the Story

Do it right, spend the money, get your three lights set up, and portray yourself in the most professional light during your digital interviews.

5. BACKGROUND

I had the privilege of working for Lufthansa German Airlines. One of the key benefits of working for an airline is the ability to flash your employee ID, hop on an aircraft, and go see the world for only a few dollars. It was an absolutely unbelievable experience—traveling the world at a young age, meeting people, and taking photographs of all the sights. Hong Kong, France, Munich, Italy—everywhere I went, I took pictures. Eventually I saved up enough money to buy a professional camera so I could capture those vibrant images of the Eiffel Tower and the Great Wall of China with a clear background. I remember taking pictures of the Alps in Switzerland and then sharing them with my family; they were amazed at how clear everything was—the subject and the background—in the photos. They actually had a hard time focusing on my profile in the picture because they were also drawn to the different mountain peaks in the background. It is amazing to be able to take really strong pictures like this, but interestingly, this is exactly what you do *not* want for your digital job interviews. The only focus should be on you, with a bland, neutral background that frames you as the main focal point.

Now you are going to have to spend a bit of money—are you ready? Here is what you'll need. I could tell you that you need to go out and buy a professional background like the ones they use at portrait studios, but I'm a Queens, New York guy, so I will tell you how to look professional for a middle-class price. What I recommend is getting a kind of photographic paper called seamless paper. It is very popular and easy to obtain. I use a company called Savage Paper; they have been in business for many years and always have a huge supply on hand. This paper will form a continuous surface behind you to cover any and all distractions. For example, let's say you are conducting your digital job interview in a conference room that faces a four-lane road. You don't want the hiring manager to see cars going back and forth, disappearing behind your head for a second before leaving the other side of the screen. To avoid this, make sure you get seamless background paper. Make sure it is a neutral color, not a bright or neon color. Use a basic, neutral shade to enhance your professional image. When you get your paper, tape it up behind you. Use a plain tape, not a huge piece of silver duct tape that will make it look like a construction project. Finally—and this is very important—*make sure it is securely fastened.* The last thing you want is your background paper falling down mid-interview. Now, the cost of a roll of true photographic seamless paper can be expensive—between $50 and $70 dollars for a 9-inch by 36-inch piece. However, I believe it is well worth the cost. It looks extremely professional and you can reuse it repeatedly for all your digital job interviews, conferences, and Skype calls. The bottom line is that using a professional background is crucial to the success of your digital job interviews.

If you don't want to spring for Savage neutral seamless paper, there is another way of doing this. Purchase a large poster board, the kind your mom used to buy you in elementary school when you had to do a math or science project with graphs and pictures.

I remember always doing my projects on white poster board when I was growing up; for your digital interviews, however, white may not be the best color for your background. These days, poster board comes in a variety of different colors with very neutral, plain backgrounds. The ultimate goal here is to pick a slightly boring shade that can serve as a nice background for your close-ups. There should be nothing distracting in the background—just your well-groomed face speaking intelligent words about what you know and what you can offer the company. So if you do not want to spend money on seamless professional photographic paper, go to your local drugstore and buy neutral-colored poster board for less than $5 dollars.

The background of your digital interview is very important. It supports everything that you are trying to convey by providing an environment and an ambience. So don't think of it merely as background. The background is the background to the camera, the background to the audio, the background to your research presentation. The minute the camera is on you want the hiring manager to think *Wow, that looks really professional* and not *Ugh, what an ugly, bright yellow; I'm already getting a headache.* Make sure you test the framing of your background before your interview. Does the background cover the entirety of what will be seen on the camera, or can you see where the poster ends and the wallpaper begins? Don't let your walls poke out on the sides. This would look extremely unprofessional. Whether you use seamless paper or a less expensive piece of poster board, make sure it is doing what you need it to do.

If you want to go all out, you can purchase the Savage seamless paper with the stand. I use one that's collapsible. It is foldable so it is easy to manage, transport, and store for future digital interviews. This is also a quicker and easier set up, as you only have to open the stand and your nice, neutral background is ready to go, as opposed to having to securely tape a poster board.

What do you do if you are really in a pinch? Let's assume (and hope!) this is not your fault. Perhaps the hiring manager accidentally double-booked his or her schedule and needs to push up your interview. You don't have time to order the seamless paper and stand on the Internet, and it's Sunday night so the local drugstore is closed. If something like this happens to you, find a piece of fabric in a neutral color and hang it from the ceiling or a curtain rod. Remember, this background should only be used as a last resort. It is still better than having your bay windows with the lawnmowers driving by outside. So now we have a few options for getting the right background for your digital interview: seamless paper, poster board, a collapsible backdrop, and, as a last resort, any neutral-colored fabric.

It should go without saying that you shouldn't destroy the look of your office or conference room with screens and tape and poster board. To make sure your backdrop stays where it's supposed to, I recommend a special kind of tape called GAFF tape. This is used by production studios and Broadway set designers. It is strong but not inordinately sticky, so you can remove it easily whenever you want to. With this product, you can put up your seamless paper easily and remove it easily without causing any damage to your walls or ceiling.

Story With a Moral

Jim was a highly accomplished computer programmer seeking a vice president of technology position in my organization. Jim was located in Iceland at the time, while I was in the United States. All was set for him to be successful in the digital interview, especially since he had a stellar background in technology. The interview started off great—the sound, video, and lighting were all perfect. However, Jim's selection for the background was not a great choice. This otherwise skilled and professional candidate hung a poster on the wall depicting female surfers in bikinis. I know it's cold is Iceland, but this was not the proper background for a digital interview!

Moral of the Story

Don't get left out in the cold by using an unprofessional background during your digital interviews. Spend a little extra money to do it right, and make your background reflect your intelligence and professionalism.

6. Putting It All Together

How cool would it be to create your own home studio and turn yourself into a CNN or *60 Minutes* broadcaster? In order to make the magic happen, let me give you a quick summary of what you need to do in order to be a real pro in the world of digital job interviewing. This applies to everyone—executives, recruiters, students, job candidates, anyone using a Webcam for a conversation or meeting should follow these easy steps. Get your name-brand camera with HD capabilities set up in your studio. Then test your lighting, background, and audio to make sure everything is in sync and looking great. When all of these parts are working together, you can tell a professional story and execute a world-class digital job interview. To review, the four primary components for success for your digital job interviews are:

1. A high-definition camera.

2. Three lights—two in front one in the back.

3. A paper or fabric background.

4. The audio components (microphone, etc.).

These four key elements will make or break your digital interviews. These technical aspects must be working together to create your masterpiece. You cannot have one more superior than the other. All your equipment must be on the same level of quality and performance to conduct a truly professional, high-quality digital interview.

Story With a Moral

Dale was a finance student in college, and I was conducting a digital interview for a financial internship at a major financial institution. Dale was my first candidate to interview. I wanted to hire Dale before he even opened him mouth. He looked professional, the audio was crisp, the lighting was perfect, and the background had obviously been professionally designed. I was sold before Dale said a word, and my initial instincts proved to be correct. About 30 minutes into the interview, I knew that Dale's preparation was an accurate indicator of his professional skills.

Moral of the Story	*Putting it all together pays off big when done correctly. Get ready to prove you will always be ready.*

7. PROFESSIONAL USERNAME

The username you select for your digital interview software is very important. Think of important people in history: George Washington, Christopher Columbus, Jackie Robinson, and so on. When we read or hear these names, we feel great respect for these strong leaders and great sports figures who have changed our world. These feelings arise just by seeing or hearing a person's name. Everything you know, feel, and understand about this person is all centered on his or her name. The minute you see or hear the name, these feelings create a mental image of the person in your mind—it only takes a second to connect his or her strong qualities with this image.

What do you think of when you hear or see the name McDonalds? Fast food, hot fries, and happy kids. How about the name of a famous actor or actress? Do you remember when you first saw him/her in the movies or on TV? Do your eyes tear up thinking about the role she played in that love story you've watched 10 times over? What is the point of all this name calling? Names have a strong impact on how we feel and think. This must be taken into account when creating your digital interview username. You want a username that evokes leadership, professionalism, and responsibility. When your interviewer looks at your username they should think, *This sounds like an excellent candidate for a job.*

Story With a Moral

Growing up in Queens, New York, I met my first friend when I was 3 years old. His name was Antanello Latnello. Now, being that we wcrc small children, this was a long name for me to say, so I decided to refer to him as "Ant." Yes, Ant, as in the little black bug. Ant and I were inseparable all the way through high school. As we got older, I would introduce my college friends to my lifelong friend, Ant, and they would give me strange looks. This is when Ant and I learned that cute, childhood nicknames cannot be carried into adulthood. It was time to change the nickname from Ant to Tony, a more grownup name to be used in social settings. I still call him Ant when I talk to him in private, but I am probably the only person in the world who calls this professional, otherwise sophisticated engineer "Ant."

Just as actors and actresses have stage names, you need to have a stage name—a username—that evokes excellence, leadership, and professionalism.

Moral of the Story	*Create a professional user-name; create a professional image.*

8. PROFESSIONAL PROFILE PICTURE

I have friends who are aspiring actors and actresses, and they have told me that one of the key things someone looking to get into commercials or Broadway must have is a portfolio. Usually this is an Internet portfolio of high quality photographs that is shown to casting directors. Similarly, it is crucial that you have a professional profile picture for your digital job interviews. When you use Skype, there is a small icon next to your username that represents you. This icon needs to be a professional-looking photograph. It should not be taken with your iPhone or taken at a photo booth with your brother or your new puppy. You do not want to start off your digital job interview with the interviewer looking you up on Skype and seeing a picture of you lying in the grass or sitting at the local bar with your friends. Instead, make sure a high-resolution, quality photograph is the first image the hiring manager associates with your name. It should be of you in professional attire, taken in front of a professional background.

After you have read this book and done all the recommended prep work, go into your broadcasting room/studio and, using a high-quality camera, take a professional-looking photograph of yourself; this will essentially represent you in your digital job interviews. If you are able, it is worth it to pay a little extra to have the photograph taken by a professional; afterward, you can also use it for your LinkedIn profile. Having a great head shot will start off your interviews on the right foot.

Story With a Moral

I was handed a resume from a senior level executive at a very large financial services company I was working for. I was instructed to interview this candidate for our leadership training program. I was happy to conduct the digital interview, as we had one slot open for the program, and the candidate's resume looked like a perfect fit. As I sat in my office waiting for the interview to begin, I searched for the candidate's profile on Skype. It wasn't hard to miss his photo—it was a LAPD mug shot from an arrest in his early days of drinking and driving. Not exactly the image you want to project for a leadership training program at a prestigious financial services organization in New York City.

Moral of the Story	*To be a star, you must look, act, and photograph like one (but not one leaving the bar at 2 a.m.).*

⑨. Clean Your Camera Lens

You want to look your best during your digital interviews. Interviewers should be able to see you clearly without any distractions. A big part of this involves removing all smudges, dirt, and dust from your camera lens prior to each interview.

When I take my son, Connor, to watch the Red Sox at Fenway Park, we usually get there an hour early to watch batting practice. Every time we're there, I always see the NESN TV cameraman cleaning his camera lens. The last time we were there he must have cleaned the lens at least 12 times. I was amazed how gently and methodically—and how often—he performed this necessary task. Upon further thought, though, I understood why he did it: who wants to be watching the World Champion Red Sox with a piece of fuzz blocking out half their screen? It is unprofessional and takes away from the main event that is being filmed. Make sure you are the main focus of your digital interview. Don't let a fuzz ball or a smudge ruin your chances of landing a job: clean your camera lens.

Story With a Moral

My wife loves to take pictures of our two children. We have so many now that I think it will take years before we can actually sit down and look at them all. One time I wanted to take a look at the pictures of our daughter, Kaitlyn, playing soccer when she scored her first goal. I knew we had pictures of this monumental event because I remember hearing my wife's camera clicking away right in my ear as I watched it all unfold.

As I was viewing these digital photos, I discovered an unfortunate error that detracts from the memory. It looks like a lightning rod is protruding from Kaitlyn's head. What happened to all the beautiful, colorful pictures I was hoping to view of my daughter scoring a goal? What happened was that someone did not properly clean the camera lens before taking the pictures. I would say who it is—but I prefer to keep the peace in my house!

Moral of the Story
Don't let a piece of hair or dust or a smudge get in the way of scoring great reviews for your digital interview. Clean your camera lens before starring in your interview. Use your manufacturers' recommended method of cleaning your camera lens. The extra few minutes are well worth the clear, clean image you'll project.

10. A Tripod Is Your Friend

When I was a kid, my sister was really into photography. She loved to take pictures of everything, and one of the key pieces of equipment she used was a tripod. She even had all the chemicals to develop her own film (by the way, this was before digital cameras, so instead of sending out her film, she created her own little darkroom). She had several different camera lenses, film cases, essentially everything she needed to be a brilliant photographer. But she insisted she needed that tripod above all else. Now, you may think that this is an unnecessary luxury, but a tripod truly helps to steady the camera. It frees up your hands and enables you to assess how you want to set up the picture. You can make sure your image is completely in focus without having to worry.

What I want you to do is get a mini tripod for your Webcam that will allow you to position the camera in the right area and focus directly on the upper portion of your body. This way, you don't have to worry about your camera hanging on the top of your monitor screen, slowly sliding down, or, even worse, crashing to the keyboard. You can purchase mini tripods relatively inexpensively, but do not get the cheapest one. Get a nice one for around $20 to $30 dollars on Amazon.com.

The camera should be positioned right in front of your monitor and it should be completely level. In order to do this, you'll need a small level (if you don't have one handy, they offer apps for smartphones that accomplish the same thing). Make sure that your digital camera is absolutely level and that it accommodates the portrait of your upper body during your digital job interviews. You don't want the camera to be focusing down at your desk or up at the ceiling.

I want you to be looking right at the camera sitting on a tripod right in front of your monitor when you conduct your digital job interviews. Yes, I know it's an additional expense for you, but you need to spend money to make money. Consider it an investment in your future career. The most critical part is that it has to be eye level. Use a tripod to get your camera at eye level so you can look your interviewer in the eye with confidence.

A tripod will also enhance your professional image. Imagine that you are watching an executive PowerPoint presentation and the projector is slightly askew. Or you are at the movie theater and the camera is slightly off-balance. It does not fill the screen correctly, and this is a distraction from the content. Likewise, it just looks sloppy and unprofessional if your image is even slightly lopsided. This is unacceptable in today's competitive job market.

S tory With a Moral

There was a time when my Dad and I used to do some woodworking. One project we made together was a toolbox. We worked all weekend and it looked beautiful. The only problem was that when we put it down on the ground, it was completely off balance. It rocked like a seesaw. It is great to think of that time my dad and I built something together in his workroom, but it would be a better memory if we had used the right tools to make the toolbox truly useful.

This also reminds me of when my wife and I purchased our first home. To help fill up all the blank walls, my wife went to Target and bought a few beautiful prints to hang up in the family room. Well, hanging them was easier said than done. I was up and down the ladder multiple times—shift a little to the left, a little to the right, now it's leaning in one direction, now it's leaning in the other direction. It was such a stressful production to line everything up and get it level. Don't let your digital interview become a stressful production. Get a tripod to hold your camera level and steady so you do not have to do any adjusting during your interview.

| Moral of the Story | *Have your camera level and steady before your interview to display a clear, focused image of your professional self.* |

11. Get the Shot: The Right Angle

It is extremely important that you understand the correct positioning of the camera and the best angle for the shot. This is crucial to performing well in a world-class digital job interview. In the world of filmmaking there is something called a high-angle shot. This is exactly what it sounds like—a shot taken from a high point. Think of being at a mall on the third floor looking down and taking a picture. This is advantageous if you are shooting down from a second story window or from a tall building. This is great if you are trying to take a picture of the streets of New York City and you are on the top floor of the Empire State building. However, this is your professional job interview—a high-angle shot is not what you want.

Alternatively, a low-angle shot expresses a point of dominance. Think of looking up from a child's point of view at an adult. You do not want to look as though you are trying to exert power over the other person or people during your digital interviews. This low-angle shot reminds me of our new puppy, Fenway. I imagine him scampering around the kitchen floor, looking up at us and seeing all these big, tall people in the kitchen looking down at him. This is a great way to train a puppy, but it is not the way you want to present yourself during your digital interview!

Another camera angle used in the film industry is the bird's-eye view. This is where you take a high angle shot and make it even more extreme until it is almost exactly overhead. I think of this angle as a police helicopter circling, looking for the criminal. Obviously you don't want your camera positioned like this during your digital interview.

Finally, there is the ground-level shot. Think of lying down in a garden to take a picture of the flowers right at their level. *This* is the angle you want for your digital interviews—exactly level with your face. This puts neither you nor the hiring manager at an inordinately high or low position. It levels the playing field. Make sure your camera is also positioned at a 90-degree angle to fill the screen with your image—the top of your head to your right shoulder to your left shoulder. This triangle comprises what is called the "money shot." The ground-level profile shot is the one you want to capture.

Story With a Moral

Whenever we go on vacation, my wife hands me the digital camera in order to take pictures. Early on, I was terrible at taking pictures of the kids. I got the sky, an arm, or a leg, but never a steady, level picture. The angles were always off, too. When I look at them now, these pictures give me quite a headache. Even when I rotate the images they still never look great. Make sure your camera is level so your image will be clearly displayed on the screen.

Moral of the Story	*A level, ground-level shot will give you a shot at getting the job.*

12. Up to Date

Before you begin your digital interviews, check the dates on all your software. You must have the most up-to-date versions of everything to perform at the highest level possible. Make sure you have the best operating system that you can afford. Make sure that you have the latest version of Skype loaded onto your computer. Check with your Internet provider to see if it's possible to increase your bandwidth for video-conferencing. I know these things are expensive, but this might be a good time to spend a little extra on better bandwidth so that your digital job interviews look extremely professional and there are no performance issues.

You want to make sure you have the latest and greatest tools available to you in order to minimize any of the risks involved in a digital job interview. The most recent Skype version is very important to have so that your sound and picture are clear and the response time is not delayed. Upgrading Skype is free and available on the Internet, so you have no excuses! Also, make sure you have the latest software in terms of your audio. Remember, I personally recommend a Blue microphone—the most efficient and effective.

You're not a second-class citizen, so why should your software be? Use the best available to show the hiring manager that *you* are the best candidate available. After you upgrade, test your new software before your digital interview. You don't want to be five minutes into the interview and not know how to change the volume off of Mute because the new software package rearranged the icons. Suddenly you're stuck on Mute, flipping through a handbook, while your interviewer is looking at your face with no sound. Not good. You and your software should be well-acquainted and performing at peak level for your digital interview.

Story With a Moral

My niece studied abroad during her junior year of college and promised she would Skype from Belgium. We tested it a few times before she left to be sure it would work. Unfortunately, a new version of Skype was released just a few days after she left the United States. The first time we tried to Skype it ended in severe frustration on both ends. Both our cameras were working but, although I could hear what she was saying, she could not hear me. Finally, after closing and reopening the application at least three times on both sides of the conversation, we got the picture and volume working. This was great for the first three minutes until the sound became so delayed that we kept interrupting each other because we did not know when the other person was speaking. Fortunately, this was a family conversation and not a professional digital interview. Still, it was an irritating experience for both of us.

Moral of the Story	*Don't let outdated technology delay your chances of getting to the next level. Have the best software to be the best candidate!*

13. POWER UP

If you plan to use your laptop, make sure your battery is fully charged. We do not recommend using battery power, but if there is no way you can keep your computer plugged into an outlet, check your laptop a few days before to see if it will hold a charge long enough for your entire digital interview. Remember, using video and add-ons drains your battery more quickly than simply typing a document in Word, so test out your battery life while running the same applications you will need for your interview. Make sure you are well in the clear. For example, if your interview is scheduled for one hour, make sure you have enough battery power for three hours. One of the worst things that could happen to you is your hard drive suddenly crashing because of the lack of battery power.

Story With a Moral

The other day I gave a presentation to a group of senior-level executives. There were about 350 people in the auditorium. I brought my laptop, which I had prepared for the presentation. I also had a backup flash drive with me, just in case anything happened. It was my understanding that the presentation would last for one hour, but I did not expect the audience to be so engaged and ask so many questions. The presentation ended up lasting two hours, but I only had about an hour and a half's worth of battery power. You can probably figure out what happened. It was a complete disaster—I was never able to show the audience the last slides with the key features of the presentation. How would you feel with 350 people awaiting your conclusion and having your battery power go out?

Moral of the Story	*Power up your laptop; power up your digital interview.*

14. Wire Up

Before you start your digital job interviews, you must check that all your wires are connected properly. It would be completely demoralizing if your digital interview failed because of a loose wire on your microphone, camera, computer, or Internet connection.

So before you begin, I want you to check and double-check every single wire in the back of your computer, in the back of your microphone, in the back of your camera—whatever electronics you will be using to communicate over the Web during your digital job interviews. I want you to follow those lines to the back of your computer and to the outlet in the wall. Make sure everything is securely connected. I do not want anyone to miss out on a job because of a loose connection, particularly since this can be easily prevented just by taking a moment of preparation.

In addition, try to avoid a rat's nest of wires during your interviews. You don't want to be tripping over or tangled in a mess of cords, unable to see which one connects to which electronic device. Almost everyone is guilty of this in their office space. When I look under my desk there are wires for the printer, the fax machine, the copy machine, the speakers, the mouse—it's a complete disaster. Avoid having tangles of wires that can accidentally pull on each other, causing disconnections or static. As well, none of these wires should be visible during your digital job interviews, so make sure they are not sitting in front of your monitor or behind you where they can be seen. Connect them neatly and securely for a neat, professional appearance during your interviews.

Most importantly, make sure that your Internet cable or DSL line is properly fit into your router. You want to ensure a quality Internet connection. There should be no connectivity issues during your interviews.

Story With a Moral

During a digital job interview I was conducting, every time the candidate put a hand on his desk or table, a crackling sound could be heard. Every time he would lean forward, the desk would move, which would vibrate in the microphone wire, causing a distracting sound. It was like someone balling up tinfoil in their hands. I couldn't understand why this person didn't go through the simple process of checking for loose connections before the interview to eliminate these kinds of distraction.

| Moral of the Story | *Don't let a crackle crack your interview—ensure you have a strong connection for a strong presentation.* |

15. Equipment Room

I am always amazed at how much equipment my son, Connor, requires to play All-Star baseball. Not only does he have his bag, his cleats, his sunglasses, his hat, his uniform, and his blackout paint for this eyes, but he also has an extra (or two) of everything, just in case something happens to his equipment during the game. So he has two or three of everything. It's insurance and assurance that we can solve anything that could possibly go wrong.

The same holds true for your digital job interview. You should always have a backup plan. You already did all the research, you networked, you established the contact, and you were called for the digital job interview—you don't want to get knocked out of the running because your camera doesn't work or your microphone sounds fuzzy or your lighting is off. You may want to consider having a Plan B in place, just in case. Have an additional camera available. Have another microphone or laptop in a position where they can be easily accessed if you need them. Obviously you want to test everything out before the interview, just in case something does go wrong. If something does go wrong, I highly recommend rescheduling your interview; but if this is the only time the hiring manager has available, you had better have a way to continue and get through it.

Story With a Moral

Just recently my son and I were at Diamond Nation, a baseball camp, for a big baseball tournament at a very competitive level. Everyone was on their A-game, making sure the team would do their best to win that number-one spot. We had the players test out all their equipment in practice the week prior to work out any issues they may have. Then, at the end of batting practice, Connor took a swing that shattered his bat right down the middle. Obviously this was not an ideal situation because he had been practicing with that bat all week; but fortunately he had brought along his back-up baseball bat. He pulled it out and was ready to go back to the plate in no time.

Moral of the Story	*When the stakes are high, have back-up equipment ready to ensure success.*

16. On-Air Sign

Studios throughout Hollywood have them, radio shows have them, and you need one for your digital interview. I'm talking about an On-Air sign. It's better to be safe than sorry. The last thing you want is someone walking into the room, calling your name, or rustling through papers in the background as you give your interview. Do everything in your power to make sure you have no interruptions during your interviews. An easy way to accomplish this is to create a makeshift On-Air sign to be placed on the closed door of your interview room/studio so everyone knows you shouldn't be disturbed.

Story With a Moral

I remember my own international digital interview for a major financial institution. They were seeking a chief marketing officer and were very interested in my background. The interview could not have been going better; I was a rock star! But then, everything suddenly went wrong. My son invited his baseball team over for some snacks and the noise was off the charts—refrigerator door banging, 12 pairs of feet in cleats clattering up the stairs to the kitchen right next to my home office. All in all, a complete disaster. This was a huge setback during the interview and I did not get the job.

Moral of the Story	*Learn from my mistake—make an On-Air sign in bold red letters and hang it on your studio/office door. Let everyone know you can't be disturbed so you can be on your digital interviewing A-game.*

17. LOCATION

Hollywood producers spend millions of dollars finding the right location to film major motion pictures. Crewmembers travel around the globe to study weather, scenery, and sunlight. Every little thing must be perfect. Days or even weeks are spent to find the right location for just a two- or three-minute scene.

I remember walking around the financial district in New York City with my wife and two children when we stumbled upon a movie production team getting ready to film a scene for *Law and Order.* The producer was looking for a stately building with Greek gothic architecture—huge rising columns and ornate pillars. Downtown New York is filled with these style buildings. We were intrigued and decided to wait to see the filming. There must have been 100 people involved— cameramen, producers, lighting people, sound crew, and various other crewmembers.

After waiting for some time they began filming and, before we knew it, they were finished! I asked one of the crewmembers, "Was that it? Five minutes of filming?!" He responded, "Yes, and we were here seven hours before the shoot to set up for these perfect five minutes." Wow! Seven hours of preparing the location just for a five-minute shoot.

If Hollywood can afford to put that much time into preparation, then so can you. Scout out a good location for your digital interview. The location sets the scene and the overall feeling for your interview. You and your interviewer should both feel that you are in a professional setting. Attire is not enough; you don't want to be wearing your $2,000 dollar suit and conducting your digital interview in the kitchen with the refrigerator behind you.

An office is typically the best location. This conveys that you are a serious professional and also mimics the setting of your interviewer, making you more connected. Sitting at your desk makes you look and feel like a confident leader. It also gives you an area to keep a pad and pen, a copy of your resume, and a sturdy surface for your microphone and camera. You are not lounging on your couch, nor are you sitting at the kitchen table with a bowl of cornflakes to the side; you are in a business setting, with everything you need laid out in front of you so that you are ready to rock your digital interview.

Story With a Moral

I was once interviewed for a television appearance in a very large studio. There must have been 50 different studio rooms from which the producer could choose. We went from room to room before she found what she was looking for—a quiet, soft setting with the right feel to convey the message of an educational, scholarly interview.

| Moral of the Story | *Location, location, location. It's important for Hollywood, it's important for business, and it's important for your digital interview.* |

18. SHADOWS

Artists often use shadows in portraits to create a special effect. This is not something you want during your digital interviews, however. When I talk about shadows, I mean things like dark bags underneath your eyes. Not a good look. Make sure you've set up the correct lighting in your home studio, which will prevent any unflattering shadows. What constitutes "correct lighting" was covered in the lighting chapter, but I truly want to emphasize the fact that you do not want to have any shadows cast on your face. Aside from purely aesthetic reasons, it can also send a psychological message that you are trying to hide something. Now, you may not think this is happening, but you need to take a close look at how your interview studio is set up and consider the natural and artificial light and how it will fall on your image.

Story With a Moral

When I was working full time for a German airline, I had the unbelievable benefit of being able to travel around the world for minimal to no cost. I was always traveling around with my camera, taking pictures of the people I visited and the sights I saw. I tried to take my shots at dusk to show the beautiful transition from light to dark. That was great for my artsy photography skills, but it is the opposite of what you want for your digital interviews. Your interviewer wants to see your natural, fully illuminated face. No shadows, no dark corners, no distractions that could offset the professional image you are trying to portray.

Moral of the Story

Make sure there are no shadows on your face during your digital interviews.

19. ASSEMBLE A CREW

All Hollywood major motion pictures have crewmembers. People who take care of the cameras, the lighting, the sound, the costumes, the scripts, the storyline—there is even a person who makes sure everyone is fed breakfast, lunch, and dinner. The same goes for producing a Broadway show. I know when we go to New York City to see a Broadway show, there are hundreds of people there prior to the start time— people setting up the cameras, lighting, microphones, music, and costumes. These types of productions have a whole crew to give support and perform at a high level.

You may want to think about having someone you can trust, readily available off-camera in order to help you perfect your digital job interview. Now, this person is not there to give you the answers during your digital job interview. His or her purpose is not to hold up cue cards for you, but he or she can help you out with issues that are out of your immediate control. He or she can make sure the lighting is correct when you are sitting down, help you with your hair and makeup, and inform other people in the house you are on an important video call. This is the person who supports you during your digital job interview just as crewmembers in Hollywood and on Broadway do. They are readily available to assist in whatever needs are necessary in order for the production to unfold professionally and smoothly, without any distractions.

What I am saying is, you don't have to go it alone. If you can find the right person who could function as an assistant or a support person to help you with your digital job interviews, why not? Just as I'm trying to help you with your digital job interviews by writing this book and doing all the research necessary to tell you how to perfect your interview. During this process, I have learned that you may need some support, that person off-camera, to help set up everything. He or she should make sure you and the set are looking professional and ready, tell others to be quiet while you are on call, and even handle unexpected issues such as the postal carrier ringing the doorbell to deliver a package. Off-camera support is key to having a smooth, successful digital job interview.

Story With a Moral

I know that in my own personal life, I could not be as successful as I am today without the help of my wife and children. Family and friends are your "crewmembers" for every task that comes up in life. I am sure when you think about your own hurdles you can imagine certain individuals who have always been there to assist you. For digital job interviews, use this word "assist" literally. Find someone who can support you off-camera during your interview to minimize your stress and make everything go smoothly. Not someone who is distracting, just someone who can remain behind the scenes, attentive and quiet, just like the crewmembers on Broadway.

Moral of the Story

Having a stage crew can improve your on-set performance.

20. X Marks the Spot

In setting up your location, think "X marks the spot." On Broadway, actors and actresses have an X to stand on to make sure they are in the correct location on the stage. Likewise, use your own "X" to mark the best place for your chair during your digital interviews. Know the perimeter of your camera span so you don't have to reach out of view during your digital interview. In addition, know the distance you should be from your camera to portray a normal, comfortable image. You do not want to be so far away that your interviewer cannot focus on your face while you are speaking. You also do not want to be so close to the camera that your interviewer can see up your nose. Mark the spot where your chair should be and test it out with a friend prior to your digital interview.

Story With a Moral

My family and I once visited Radio City Music Hall—the world famous home of the Rockettes and the Christmas Show. Living in Trumbull, Connecticut, the trip to New York City is a short train ride away. My wife, Kathleen, always loves visiting the city, and this time we were going to take a backstage tour of Radio City. It was interesting to find out how the real magic of the show comes together behind the scenes.

When we finally got to stand on the stage of Radio City Music Hall, a Rockette was there to greet us and answer any questions we had. I noticed there were "X"s marked all over the stage in different colors. I had to ask the question, "What are all those X's on the stage?" She answered, "The X tells us where to stand so the audience can see us. When we want to stand and kick in a straight line, we all have to stand on our X's. It works great, no one can see the marks, and our performance looks perfect!"

Remember this story when you are preparing for your digital interviews. Get a piece of white paper or some tape and place it on the perfect spot where your chair needs to be situated. Skype a friend and test out the spot until you are centered. Ask your friend if you look professional: Are you centered and visible at all times? If the answer is yes, you're ready to go!

Moral of the Story	*Be like the Rockettes. Mark the spot and be the star of your digital interview.*

21. Portrait

When you're taking a photograph, what is the difference between portrait and landscape in terms of their focal points? I remember going out West and looking out at the Grand Canyon and taking out my camera to take a picture. It was just so amazing that even when I set my digital camera to landscape, it did not do it justice. The Grand Canyon has so much beauty and is so vast that it is impossible to capture everything it has to offer merely through a digital photograph. I don't want this to happen to you during your digital job interviews! Don't let the image your interviewer sees to be so vast that it is difficult for him to focus. So, don't think landscape photography; think portrait: first Communion photograph, elementary school photograph, prom portrait—photographs that are focused on *you*. These are the complete opposite of the photographs I have taken at the Grand Canyon that contain multiple areas of focus. I want you to be the focus of your digital job interview. I call this the "triangle of love." It goes from shoulder to shoulder to the top of your head with just a few inches of clearance all the way around. This is the optimal way to frame your face during your interviews.

Think of your high school yearbook photograph. Open up your wallet and take a look at your driver's license photo. These are the images you want to replicate in your digital interviews. The focus of your digital job interview is you—your face, your facial expressions, not the rest your body—so that you can make that emotional connection with the interviewer. Frame your face so your interviewer can feel this emotional connection and focus on you.

S tory With a Moral

When I was in Rome I took what I thought were some beautiful shots of the Vatican, but when I got home and looked at them, they were just too big. They had no focal point. Why should people want to look at my pictures when they were just massive scenes? After that, when I was traveling in the United States, I focused very tightly on some wildflowers in the mountains of Wyoming. I found one particularly beautiful flower and focused in as best as I could. It happens to be one of the best pictures I have ever taken. It contains no distractions. When people look at that photograph, the flower is the one and only thing they see. Many people have told me what a beautiful photo it is. That is exactly what I want the hiring manager to say about your digital job interview: "What a wonderful image, perfectly framed." The portrait of your face that you create through your Webcam should be perfectly centered, perfectly focused.

Moral of the Story	*Use the triangle of love—be the center of your portrait during your digital job interviews.*

22. Toastmasters International Is Your Friend

I have been a Toastmasters member for many years and I absolutely love it. Toastmasters International is actually a great way for you to prepare for your digital job interviews. If you have not heard of Toastmasters International, it is a worldwide organization that is relatively inexpensive to join and has chapters all across the United States. Its mission is to help people perfect their speaking abilities and presentation skills. You can even ask them to videotape you while you are going through your speeches. This is a wonderful and extremely effective way to help get you ready for your digital job interviews.

I suggest you go to their Website, *www.toastmasters.org*, and find a club that is near you. I believe the fee is less than $100 dollars for a year-long membership. Make sure you join a club that will be able to videotape you. Review the videos right away so that you can get immediate feedback. This feedback will significantly enhance and improve your interviewing skills.

You may want to give a speech relating to your interview so you can use this time to plan what you will say during your digital job interviews. Remember, the whole point of joining Toastmasters is for you to increase your confidence and your ability to stand up and speak professionally. It provides a safe, supportive environment in which to practice speaking and the opportunity to be videotaped. Use this inexpensive resource to enhance your communication skills and perfect your digital job interviewing skills.

Story With a Moral

I remember when I had to give an executive level presentation to outside investors. At the time, I was a member of the International Toastmasters club in Stamford, Connecticut. The Toastmasters meeting that I was attending was a week prior to my executive level investor meeting. I practiced by giving the speech that I was planning to give to the investors (without the confidential and proprietary information, of course). It was an eye-opening experience in terms of what I learned about my presentation form. By participating in Toastmasters and getting feedback, I can guarantee you that my performance during the live investor meeting was 150 times better than if I had not gone to Toastmasters. The evaluation feedback I received made the presentation that much better. It was the opportunity to actually see what I was doing wrong (via the videotapes) before the actual presentation, that allowed me to excel. Toastmasters helped me see those little and no-so-little things that needed improvement, all of which helped drive the message home during my investor meeting.

Moral of the Story

Join Toastmasters to boost your confidence and perfect your digital job interview skills.

23. Tune In

You cannot change the channel during your digital job interview. The star of the show is you, and you must maintain your hiring manager's full attention. You want to make sure that you are well-prepared for each interview, just as an actor or actress must be prepared for each role. A great way to prepare is to visualize exactly how you want your digital interview to go. Do you want to be the star of a comedy like *Saturday Night Live*? It's a funny show, but emulating it probably wouldn't get you the job. I would suggest watching *60 Minutes* to see how the program is put together. Not only how the actors/reporters are projecting their words, but their mannerisms, the background, the lighting, the sound, and the stories they present. Watching *60 Minutes* is a great way to learn how to conduct your digital interviews.

I find this show intriguing, but when you think about it, there is not much to it in terms of bells and whistles. The main focus is the reporter, sitting there and talking about a particular story or topic. There is no elaborate background, no special effects, and no cartoons running across the screen. It is a simple backdrop with very simple lighting, and the main focus on the speaker.

After you watch a few episodes of *60 Minutes*, search for *Harvard Business Review* on YouTube. You can watch Harvard interviews for free—you can't beat that! Watch how these professionals conduct their presentations and interviews and then emulate them in your digital job interviews. They are collected, intelligent, and professional. No frills, no comedies, just straightforward but emotionally invested conversation. Watch these shows to think ahead and plan what you want your digital job interview to be like. Major news shows and major interviews with corporate leaders and academic professionals do an absolutely phenomenal job in preparing people for interviews just by providing an example for people to listen to.

Story With a Moral

I was asked to do an interview with Fox News and this was to be the first time I was on television. In order to prepare, I watched the professionals: *60 Minutes*, the national news, the *Harvard Business Review*. I observed these broadcasts and others to learn how I should behave during my own interview. I paid attention to how the interviewer and interviewee connected and spoke to one another, and took it away for my own studies. So I'm not just coming up with this idea and telling you to try it out—I have actually done it and it has worked for me. If it can work for me, it will work for you in order to be successful in your digital job interview.

Moral of the Story

Practice by watching the experts. Learn from the best—it's free!

24. Honey

Okay, so you made it through the resume-writing process, garnered the attention you needed, and now you are all set up for your digital job interview—lighting ready, backdrop ready, research ready. Everything is good to go. Now that both your equipment and your mind are fully prepared, the last step you need to take is to make sure your voice is fully prepared. To soothe your throat, take a teaspoon of honey about an hour prior to your digital job interview. This will resolve any scratchiness or soreness and help you sound much better. I also recommend this in *The Official Phone Interview Handbook* for people who are giving phone interviews. This makes your voice sound so much clearer, which is exactly what you want. Obviously, your voice is essential to giving a great interview. In order to ensure that you are "in voice," that little teaspoon of honey really helps.

Story With a Moral

I remember conducting a digital job interview for a senior-level position in a financial services company during which, every few minutes, the other person cleared his throat and reached for a glass of water. This was a real distraction. Imagine telling someone about your background, pausing to clear your throat, continuing to tell someone about your education, pausing to clear your throat, then describing your experience and—wait

for it—clearing your throat yet again.
Even just reading this text it is extremely
distracting. The focus of your interview should
be on you and the other person, sharing skill
sets and ideas, connecting on an emotional
level, full of compelling content, not coughs.

Moral of the
Story

*Don't be constantly clearing your
throat during your digital job
interviews—get that scratchy itch
out of your voice with a teaspoon
of honey.*

25. Write Your Script

Preparation will win you your digital job interview. Think about anyone you have seen perform on camera—actors, actresses, news reporters, and so on. They all have a script. They learn it, practice it, and often have it behind the camera during filming. So why not write your own script for your digital interview? Write out your proposition to get a sense for how it sounds. Does it stick to a main point? Does it proclaim your skills loud and clear? Write a script that will highlight why this manager should hire you.

What I want you to do is go to your local office supply store and purchase some presentation sheets. They're slightly expensive, but well worth it. Write down the top key points you want to bring up during your digital interview. Make sure you write neatly and clearly—you may want to consider using different colors to indicate different topics; just be careful you don't turn it into an arts and crafts project. Post these papers right behind your camera. Consider these pages your own personal teleprompter—they won't be seen on camera, but they are easily visible to you so you can stay calm, organized, and professional. Following is an example of a digital interview "teleprompt," with the main topic of leadership:

Leadership:

▷ Manage 150 people: vice presidents, directors, and managers.

▷   Yearly reviews by staff and peers in the 100th percentile in leadership.

▷   Style: roll-up-your sleeves executive leader; train with the team.

You could have more bullet points in a different color. Post this at eye level behind your camera so you can easily look up and think about what you want to say about your leadership skills and experience. It will look as though you are looking at the camera, but, really, you are looking at the notes behind it.

Don't go crazy and cover your entire office with presentation sheets; keep it subtle—clean, precise, clear notes posted outside the range of your Webcam. This is a great way to jog your memory in case you get nervous. Having your notes to fall back on will help you be a more confident interviewee.

Story With a Moral

I remember sitting in a grand auditorium at the headquarters of American Express. I was always amazed at how well the executive leadership team presented. I arrived early to get a good seat up front to watch how these top executives presented at a global conference. This presentation was to be broadcasted around the world, so they needed to have the best quality equipment— professional lighting, high-tech cameras, and a producer who was connected with the camera people. I noticed the presenters were very good at speaking without any papers or note cards in front of them. Looking around the auditorium, I noticed a plasma screen behind the audience that wasn't turned on before the start of the presentation. It was then that I realized that when the presenters were looking at the audience, they were really looking at the multiple plasma screens indicating all of their speaking notes. The presentation was impressive, articulate, and clear.

| Moral of the Story | *Be an executive president—have your script posted behind your Webcam.* |

26. READ THE SCRIPT

Make sure you study your script before each digital interview. Do you know your lines? Just as an actor or actress in a movie does, you have to know your lines. If you don't, it wastes time and makes you look unprofessional. There are no cuts or retakes in your digital interview. Know what you need to say before you start your interview. Are you prepared to answer the interviewer's questions? Have you reviewed the job description? Do you know the goals and accomplishments of this company? Read the script, know your lines, and rock your digital interview on the first—and only—take.

Story With a Moral

I can remember being incredibly confused during one digital interview I conducted. The candidate's story made absolutely no sense—there was no connection to the position, and the time line of his professional story was difficult to follow. I couldn't understand how surfing in Hawaii and selling hot dogs in New York City were remotely connected to designing mobile applications for the position. I tried hard to connect the dots, but I could never really connect with the candidate. Confusing the hiring manager with your story is not a great way to get a job.

Moral of the Story

Make your script pay off: tell your story cogently, clearly, and concisely, and you will ace the interview!

27. GET COMFORTABLE

The day I graduated from St. John's University my parents said they wanted to buy me a new suit so I would be properly dressed for my job interviews. After a few hours of selecting the right interview suit and getting it tailored, we walked out of Dadson's, a men's suit shop in Queens, New York, with my new, professional outfit. My dad said some wise words to me: "It will take a few times of wearing your new suit to interviews before you get comfortable in it. You'll become more and more confident and professional in your suit with time." This turned out to be true. The first time I wore my new suit, it felt like a straight jacket. After years of wearing shorts, jeans, and sweats to class it felt a bit weird to be so dressed up. I felt uncomfortable and awkward, as though I had poison ivy all over my body. But fortunately my dad was right. After a few wearings I felt good in my professional attire and I looked great (or so said my mom and sisters). It fit me like a glove.

Just as getting comfortable in a new suit does, getting comfortable in front of a camera takes some time. I want you to turn on your computer, turn on your camera, and just look at yourself. What do you like about what you see? What don't you like? Are you stiff and uneasy? Do you look calm and professional, like a news anchor? Or rigid and stiff, like a ship's anchor? Spend some time in front of the camera before your first digital interview to get used to being on camera. Now, I do not mean you should become so comfortable that you let your guard down and act silly. I want you to find your professional camera persona—sharp, clear, witty, and intelligent. Find the camera image that will make you look great and feel great so that you will do great.

Just as my dad said, I needed time for my suit to become a part of me; you will need time for your Webcam image to become a part of you.

Story With a Moral

I remember the first time I wore my new suit. It was to an interview at an investment banking firm in New York City. Unfortunately, when I tried it on beforehand, I looked and felt uncomfortable to the extreme. My suit pants were stiff, and the suit jacket seemed to chafe everywhere. In college I wore sweats, shorts, and T-shirts almost every day. But now I was trying to be Mr. Investment Banker, with an obviously new custom suit, feeling very uncomfortable indeed. I needed to quickly get comfortable in the suit before my big interview, so I wore it around the house. The more I wore my suit, the more comfortable I became in it; it became my second skin. By the time my interview rolled around, I both looked and felt great.

Moral of the Story	*Your camera persona is the identity you portray to your interviewer. Get comfortable in your new interviewing clothes in order to ace your interview.*

28. CRITICS

In the movie business, one way to know whether your show is performing well is by reading the reviews written by critics. A critic has a point of view that is independent of the actors, actresses, producers, and directors who work on the show. He or she offers a (usually) objective perspective regarding the quality of the performance. For your digital interviews, you need to be your own worst critic. You need to be brutally honest about how you're doing. Don't lie to yourself—after all, where will that get you? Certainly not to a better interview and a new career.

The hard part is how, exactly, do you critique what you are doing and how you sound? Are you emotionally connected with the other person during these interviews, or are you a zombie? Be honest.

A useful exercise for this is to practice your digital interviews using Skype. I want you to dress up, prepare, and connect with someone on the other end—a friend or professional colleague—to conduct a mock digital job interview. This person shouldn't be a family member; you need someone objective who will tell you the truth, even if it is hard to hear. You need a gentle but 100-percent honest critic to tell you everything you are doing wrong. This is the only way to get better, unfortunately. If you can't think of anyone, you can e-mail me at *executive@phoneinterviewpro.com* and I will conduct a mock digital phone interview with you to critique your skills. But the less expensive way to do it is find somconc who will spend time with you and tell you the truth. As crucial as it is for you to be your own worst critic, you must also hear what the real critics have to say. Practice your digital interview in a safe environment with a friend or professional colleague before you go live.

Story With a Moral

As a chief marketing officer I had a young senior vice president reporting to me. I was trying my best to advise him, but he was not open to criticism. It wasn't criticism against him, but constructive criticism to help him improve. Unfortunately, he avoided the critics, he avoided the truth, and he was never able to solve his leadership issues. Thus, he was never able to progress in his career.

I want you to be successful in every one of your digital job interviews. I want you to master Skype better than anyone else and I want you to improve. I need you to listen to the truth. Surround yourself with truth-tellers. Asking people to be honest with you is the only way to have a long-running show.

| Moral of the Story | *Be your own worst critic to become your very best.* |

29. "THREE, TWO, ONE...
AND WE'RE LIVE!"

Movies and TV shows are edited and re-edited before they are finalized and released. You need to remember that the digital interview is not like this. The interview is live, so there's no time for reviewing and editing before "releasing" your interview to your potential future employer. There are no second chances, so you need to be able to perform under pressure in the present.

When I was a boy, my father and I would often journey into New York City for the day. I always loved holding my father's hand as we admired the great city buildings and all the fascinating people. One time we were walking down Fifth Avenue; it was a Saturday afternoon and the city was filled with various people rushing around, most of whom seemed to be tourists. As we stood on the street corner waiting to cross a main intersection, a older Italian gentleman approached my dad. He looked as though he were lost, with a map in hand and a look of confusion on his face. He asked my father, "How do you get to Carnegie Hall?"

I stood next to my father and looked up, waiting for his response.

"My good fellow, the only way to get to Carnegie Hall is to practice, practice, practice." The gentleman looked stunned and we proceeded to cross the street.

This same humorous advice applies to your digital interview. The only way to get ready for a live digital interview is to practice, practice, practice. The more often you do, the better you will become.

Before your live digital interview, record yourself conducting an interview and then review. How do you look? How do you sound? What image are you projecting? Do you like what you see? These are all important questions to ask yourself. Look for mistakes and think of how you can correct them. This is your only chance to correct your mistakes and become a better digital interviewer.

Story With a Moral

My son Connor is a big baseball fan. He loves the Red Sox, and he loves playing for his local baseball team in Connecticut. After every game we "debrief" on his performance as we drive home. We discuss what when well, what did not go well, and what he still needs to work on. It is up to Connor to practice every day to cut down on the mistakes and increase his skill. The only way to increase skill (especially in baseball) is practice, practice, practice. There simply is no substitute.

| Moral of the Story | *Live is live—there is no going back. What you say and do during your digital interview is all the hiring manger will see of you. Minimize your mistakes and increase your skills with practice, practice, practice.* |

30. No Editing Crew

You have read about some similarities between digital interviews and movie casts/Broadway actors and actresses, but now you're going to learn about something that is different. In your digital interview you have no cast and no editing crew. You are the star and you share the spotlight with only one other person—your costar, the hiring manager. So remember, your interview is what it is, and there's no going back for do-over's. No matter how hard you try, it is impossible to go back in time, so remember that there is no editing crew waiting in the wings. Whatever happens, happens. You don't have the luxury of having an editing team go back and review your interview. You need to be on your A-game every single time.

The only way to prevent errors from happening during your digital job interviews is to be prepared. The more you prepare, the less likely it is you will make any serious errors and not get to the next step, the face-to-face interview. Now, don't get too stressed out about this. No matter how hard you prepare you have to be aware that things may not go exactly the way you predicted; you may have to improvise a bit, and you may make some small mistakes. This is okay—you're only human. For example, a friend of mine was interviewing for a high-level project manager job at a Fortune 500 company and he said to me, "I wish your book were out already so I knew how to expect the unexpected in my digital interview. I was using Skype, and for the entire 60 minutes I was staring at a green screen! The other person could see and hear me, but I could only see this green screen."

If something like this happens to you, go with the flow. Try not to let your stress show when things go wrong because, believe me, they will; there is too much technology and too many uncontrollable factors involved. Just be prepared that no matter how much you prepared, things will go wrong.

The other day I was watching a documentary about Navy SEALs on The History Channel. They practiced jumping out of helicopters in SCUBA gear and repeated many drills for their mission. Then, when the day of reckoning came, they were outnumbered and had to change their entire plan. They had to react on the spot, but because they had prepared, they were ready for the unknown. They knew there was no going back, so they charged ahead with the skills they had prepared. It is the same for your digital interview. Things you did not expect may happen, but remember there is no going back, no editing team, so forge ahead with the skills you have prepared. Do the very best that you can.

Movie stars perform seamlessly in their films because they have an editing crew that can cut the film when they make a mistake in their lines and go back and redo it. In your digital interview there are no redos. Don't get down on yourself if, after all your preparation, you fumble your words a little bit. Think of it as a Broadway show: No matter how long and how hard one practices, sometimes mistakes happen. Actors and actresses deal with any in-the-moment changes professionally and so should you. Be professional, keep your cool, and make your point.

Story With a Moral

Think about the movies you like to watch and look into what makes them so interesting. Is it the characters, the action, the visuals, or the theme? Whatever it is, keep that element in mind and try to make it one of your digital interview strengths. Make your digital interview something *you* would like to watch—interesting, exciting, easy on the eyes. Just don't treat your live digital interview like a Disney movie. There is no Tinkerbell in the world of digital interviewing. You can't go back and edit your take with a little bit of pixie dust. It is only you and the person behind the camera, one on one, so make sure you get a great review.

| Moral of the Story | *Don't depend on Tinkerbell; don't look for the editing crew, because there isn't one.* |

31. Don't Be a Diva

Hollywood is filled with actors and actresses who think they are bigger and better than they really are. They think they are the most important part of the show—more important than the stage crew, more than the directors, and more than the audience. Some actors and actresses even have crazy clauses in their contracts like allowing only green M&Ms in their dressing room, making some poor soul separate them out into a specific bowl.

Don't be a diva during your digital job interviews. People do not want to hire people who think they are better than everyone else, especially if the interviewer is the person who is going to be your boss. Most people do not like or get along with people who have big egos. Rather, they want to work with intelligent, responsible team players. Don't be a diva. You want to be professional and humble during all your interviews. Your goal for your interview is not to show how wonderful you are, but to display how helpful you are, how kind you are, how intelligent and knowledgeable you are, and how excited you are about the position.

The interview cannot be all about you; it has to be about them, too. Divas always have trouble focusing on other people. They have trouble connecting emotionally with other people because their world consists of them and only them. Divas are self-absorbed—it's all about what they are they doing and what they want. They forget to consider how they affect and are affected by the people around them. A diva cannot relate to other people. But digital job interviews must also be about the other person. Connecting and communicating with others on a human level is already difficult through a screen, so don't add diva qualities to this challenge.

You have to focus in on the other person during your digital interview. Hear what that person has to say and understand his problem. Yes, he does have a problem. The problem is that looking for a talented person like you is a complex and difficult task. You have to understand and solve his problem(s) with your skill set. Don't focus on what you think is great about you in a general sense—focus on what is great about you that is going to benefit the company. You have to talk in terms of the other person and the environment you are trying to enter. Tell him how your educational background and professional experience is going to solve his problem. Divas think the world revolves around them; successful job interviewers know they must correctly place themselves in the puzzle that is the company and its problems.

When you are practicing for your digital interview, think about how you feel. Are you truly concerned about the organization's issues and problems? Are you emotionally connected to the person on the other side of the screen? If you don't feel any empathy regarding the problem, I suggest you stop for a moment, gather your thoughts, and figure out why you feel disconnected. Digital interviewing is all about helping the other person and solving her problem(s). I know you have worked hard preparing for this interview. You are highly educated, you read this book, you practiced all the skills I recommended, but you must leverage all of this to make *them* look good, not just you. If you can prove how your skills will make this company look good, then you have nailed it. Be connected to and concerned about the hiring manager's problems. This proves you are emotionally invested and motivated to be the best candidate for this position.

Story With a Moral

When I was an executive running a major digital marketing company, there were many talented people that I had the honor of interviewing from some of the top schools in the nation. All of these candidates appeared absolutely perfect on paper—high GPAs with great backgrounds. When I began conducting digital interviews for a number of these candidates, I knew within the first few minutes if it was about the position or just about their own situation. I could tell if they were proud and pompous of their own qualities—proving their own greatness, but not all that interested in what they could bring to the company. I could tell, almost instantly, if they were only looking out for themselves not caring about others.

The person I eventually selected came from a good school, not an Ivy League school, and his work experience background was okay, but not overly impressive. What set him apart from the others was that he came across in his digital job interview as hungry to succeed. He came across as being hard working, diligent, and tenacious. He managed to communicate through the screen that he was one who wanted to learn and would be of great value to the organization. There was an immediate connection over the Web during his digital job interview, and so I knew I would make this young person an offer.

Moral of the Story   *Don't be a diva—be empathic and make a connection.*

32. Costume Design

Costume design is an important part of any motion picture production. It communicates essential character traits. Likewise, you need to have a well-assembled "costume" for your digital interview. Remember, you don't have a film editor. What you do and say is done—no going back. This also applies to how you dress. You have one take and one take only, so make it a good one.

Think of how elaborate Broadway costumes are. They transform the actors into completely different characters. Every play and every motion picture has a costume designer who allows the performers to become someone or something completely different. These costumes create an image that brings the story to life. You don't have a costume designer for your digital interview but you still need to bring character and charisma to your story.

▷ **Hair and makeup artist:** You need to make sure your hair is well-groomed and you have the proper makeup on to look your best on camera. Makeup can and should be used by both men and women. Make sure you wash your face first. You don't want the lighting to reflect off oily spots on your face. Then use a translucent powder to help keep the shine down. Have your hair done neatly, pulled back from your face so you do not have an urge to play with it. Both men and women should have their nails neatly trimmed and manicured (no garish polish, please) in case their hands are visible on camera.

▷ **Clothing:** You need to have a costume designer. This person can be you or it can be a shopping assistant, a fashion consultant, your tailor, or a dressmaker. If you are buying new clothes or having something made, make sure it looks professional. Look in the mirror at the shop and ask yourself, *Do I look like an A-plus job candidate? If I saw myself on video would I feel confidence and intelligence coming through the screen?* If you are interviewing for a professional or C-level position, your "costume" should consist of a perfectly fitting, clean-cut suit. You need to be dressed up for your digital job interviews as if you were going for a face-to-face interview. This will make you look and feel professional, putting yourself and your viewers in the correct setting.

▷ **Jewelry:** If you are going to wear jewelry make sure it is appropriate—no big diamonds that are going to catch the light and create a glare, and no dangly earrings that are going to rattle when you turn your head. Hollywood costume designers are hired because they pay meticulous attention to detail. You need to do the same for your digital job interview. Leave your Mickey Mouse wristwatch behind when you are interviewing for an executive position. Dress professionally and accessorize professionally—everything counts when you're on camera! Your attire must match your character and also the traits of a person who would excel at your desired position.

Story With a Moral

Think of yourself as a costume designer for a major motion picture. You want to make sure everything looks and fits the part of the job you are applying for. The wrong costume can confuse people and take away from your persona.

I can remember when I was going for an interview for a senior-level position and my very expensive high-quality watch was in the shop. The only watch I could find when I was running out the door was my Timex. A very cool, five-dollar watch that I bought at the Timex outlet so I could keep track of time when my son and I go to play catch at the park. I was sitting face-to-face with my interviewer in my custom-made suit when I suddenly realized he was focused on my watch. This accessory confused him. Why would this top executive candidate, looking so polished, educated, and successful, be wearing a Timex watch? He could tell this one piece of my "costume" did not fit the picture, and this distracted him from my professional presentation. This last-minute flaw in my costume design cost me major points during my interview, as it did not fit the character I was trying to portray.

| Moral of the Story | *Choose your interview "costume" carefully and be the "character" you want your interviewer to see! The right accessories, perfectly paired with your attire, will enhance your brand.* |

33. CLEAR SCREEN

You don't want any unnecessary distractions during your digital job interviews, so a clear screen is the best screen to have. You are already under enough pressure to perform well; you don't need a distraction in the form of a cluttered screen to take your attention off your performance.

You want to make sure any unnecessary software is turned off. That means you're logged out of IM (Instant Messaging), e-mail, and so on. Your fans and friends can wait! Nothing should be popping up on your screen during your digital interviews. Even if you think you can ignore it, your eyes will naturally dart to whatever pops up on your screen, and your interviewer will notice. In addition, remove any external decorations from your computer. A number of my students have different things hanging off their laptops—sticky notes, cute stickers, and so on. My daughter has little teddy bears hanging all over her monitor. This is cute for an 8 year old, but it is not cute for a professional trying to get a job.

Have a clear screen for your digital interview. It is a simple preparatory step that can have a significant impact on your interview. Do not let anything detract from your focus on your digital job interview.

Story With a Moral

S I remember conducting a digital job interview for a director position and, halfway through the interview, I saw things falling down in front of the camera. I was very confused—it seemed to be raining teddy bears! Apparently, the candidate had a number of old stuffed animals on top of a ledge, and they were falling down right in front of the camera. This was very distracting for both of us and it really disrupted the interview.

Moral of the Story	*Clear your screen, clear your mind, and keep your focus and concentration.*

34. Grooming Tips

Every great actor, news anchor, political figure and celebrity has a makeup artist. Many women spend hours doing their makeup before venturing out of the house every day. Similarly, looking great is a big part of the digital interviewing process. The better and more prepared you look, the better the initial connection. This doesn't mean you don't have to be smart, professional, experienced, and skilled to get the job, but it does help to look good. Don't be *too* focused on looking good; it's simply one part of the puzzle of having a successful digital interview.

There are four key areas of grooming to focus on for your digital job interviews:

1. **Hair:** Visit a salon or barber shop before you go "on air" for your interview. Your face is the focal point of the interview, and your hair is a big part of this. You want your hair to look fresh, natural, neat, and clean—in a word, professional. Stray hairs or hair falling in your face will be a distraction to the hiring manager; don't lose out to hair that's out of place!

2. **Skin:** Wash your face thoroughly before your digital interview. You don't want to have a greasy face that will look shiny on screen. Women: professional but subtle makeup will go a long way in your interviews, especially with all the lights that will be on you.

3. **Hands:** Consider how your nails look. Are your nails trimmed and clean, not jagged and rough? Men, it is okay to get a manicure! I am not suggesting you wear nail polish; just get them cleaned up. Wash your hands and moisturize them so that they look smooth and well-tended. On my weekends I often work on my car, on the lawn, or on the house, and I could spend hours getting my hands clean for the next day. To avoid this, I wear gloves. Take care of your hands and keep them youthful and clean. Women, if you like to wear nail polish, don't pick a bright or too-dark color that will be a distraction during your interview. Pick clear polish or a neutral, natural color that enhances your professionalism and harmonizes with your skin tone and outfit.

4. **Teeth:** Clean, shiny white teeth are a must. Make your smile something the interviewer wants to look at, not something that makes her cringe. Practice good hygiene by brushing your teeth and tongue before your interview.

Story With a Moral

I was once asked to be interviewed on a new TV show called *On Your Watch with Christine Giordano*. The interview was to take place in East Hampton, New York, but I live in Trumbull, Connecticut, a long distance away. I knew it was going to be 95 degrees that day, and I knew I would have to take the car and a ferry. So, two days before the interview, I made sure I got a haircut, had my nails manicured, and had my suit pressed. I asked my wife to pack me a travel bag even though I would only be gone for five hours. I brought my suit, a toothbrush, shoes, and facial wipes to keep my face clean and shine-free. I even brought some hair gel to make sure I didn't have a hair out of place—I didn't want my hair to be a distraction on the show!

Moral of the Story	*There are many little things that add up to that one big thing of acing your digital interview—looking good for your "close-up" is one of them.*

35. THE POWER OF COLOR

Color has a profound effect on mood. The colors you wear affect the overall feeling and energy you project outward, to others. They also affect how you feel about yourself. Color is a kind of unwritten, nonverbal language that can have a significant impact on your digital job interviews. Think about the effect color has on you as an individual. Think about how you feel when you look up at an overcast sky and you see gray clouds. Does this make you feel happy or sad? Compare this to seeing a meadow of vibrantly colored wildflowers. There is a significant difference in terms of the mood that these two scenes evoke in your mind and in your soul. For your digital interviews, you must use the best, most effective color contrasts between your skin, your wardrobe, your background, and your lighting. All of these things need to be in balance and reflecting the same mood.

Think about what can happen with the wrong color combination. What kind of mood would you be in if you turned on your videoconference meeting and you saw the other person in a red dress standing in front of a red background? She would look like a floating head in a sea of red! You don't want this to happen to you. You want to project the right image by leveraging the power of color to set the mood for your interview.

The best colors to use for your background are, again, neutral shades that are easy on the eyes. Think beige, tan, pale gray, or slate blue. These colors work best as long as what you are wearing is enhanced by, and not engulfed by, these backgrounds. In my research, slate blue has proven to work best; obviously, if you are planning on wearing a suit of this color, that won't work for you. So make sure you consider your overall color scheme in terms of coordinating your outfit with your background.

You also want to make sure that the colors selected do not cause eyestrain on the other person's monitor. You'll want to avoid stark whites and overly bright colors because they are not optimum for viewing. These colors can be hard on the eyes and cause headaches. A background of pure white can be a bit tough on the eyes. Similarly, you also do not want neon colors, which can make you look as though you were in an Austin Powers movie. Do not use a color that will reflect light back at the camera and create a harsh image.

To help you get the right mood, think of a calm, tranquil scene and what colors tend to go along with it. For example, think of a green field with trees and beautifully colored flowers. Can you picture the colors that complement each other in this setting? Now use this imagery to leverage the power of color that will create a professional mood and help focus the attention on you. A nice, neutral background with a neutral wardrobe that does not compete with the background is the way to go. Again, stay away from white or too-bright colors.

In addition, consider the color of anything that may appear on your screen during your videoconference. For example, perhaps you are a basketball fan and you have a brand-new NBA signed basketball on a shelf in your office. This orange ball is going to stick out against your serene background and be a distraction. You want color to enhance the story you are trying to tell. You want the colors to be in harmony with each other, all working together to reflect you and your strong, professional assets that make you a great job candidate.

Story With a Moral

I once had the opportunity to interview a senior leader for research on ego management. This highly regarded individual in the field of marketing technology agreed to a digital interview so I could gain insight into how she leads her company. I was on the East Coast and she was on the West Coast. Everything was going great—engaging, articulate conversation—until she placed her hands on top of her desk in full view of the Webcam. For some reason, she was wearing neon purple nail polish. From that point on, I was completely distracted by the color of that nail polish. It was like a beacon, drawing me in and pulling my attention away from the topic at hand. Now, since I had my Webcam set up correctly to show my eyes, it was obvious I was continually glancing at her hands. More than halfway through the digital interview she was kind enough to tell me that, over the weekend, her 9-year-old daughter had painted her nails, and in the rush of normal life, she had forgotten to remove it before coming to work that day. We proceeded with the interview and I was less distracted, but this still threw off the flow of our entire videoconference. The bright color lured my eyes and my attention, which had a detrimental impact on our conversation.

| Moral of the Story | *Employ a balance of colors to keep the interviewer focused on what is important—you and your career.* |

36. Show Skills, Not Skin

I know I already mentioned this briefly, but make sure you are professionally dressed for your digital interviews. You would not believe the number of job candidates who conduct digital interviews in their pajamas. This is simply unacceptable. You must dress as though you were going to a face-to-face interview. This means long skirts, long sleeves, covered shoulders, buttoned shirts, and high necklines. This is not a day at the beach or a night out clubbing with your friends; it's a professional endeavor. Showing too much skin on a digital interview will not help your chances of obtaining a rewarding position. At the risk of stating the obvious, skin can be a distraction, and you will be perceived as unprofessional. Less is better; don't tarnish your reputation—make a great impression!

Story With a Moral

Have you ever walked through the financial district in a major city? What are a majority of the businessmen and -women wearing? They are wearing buttoned-up shirts or blouses, jackets, ties, dress pants, suits. Now, have you ever walked though a popular bar on the weekend? What are a majority of the patrons wearing? Tank tops, shorts, tee-shirts, miniskirts, sneakers, more revealing clothing. Think about this clothing comparison. The professionals are covered up, displaying leadership and maturity. The people at the bar—they aren't there to work; they're out to have fun. This is okay for them, but not for you on your digital interviews.

Moral of the Story	*Show more skills and less skin on your digital interviews.*

37. Write Your Worries Away

The number-one reason for failure during digital interviews is self-inflicted: worrying about the interview itself. Well, here's a secret: worrying can be avoided! Here are two simple steps to help you do just that:

1. The night before your digital interview, tap into your subconscious. I want you to repeat this phrase fives times before you go to bed: "I will do a great job on my digital interview."

2. Write your worries away. I want you to take a piece of paper and pen and write down what you are worried about before your digital interview. Not looking good, too much pressure, saying the wrong thing, whatever. Write down all your worries and then throw out the piece of paper before each interview. Throw your worries away, literally! I can guarantee that if you are honest with yourself and you write down the issues that are most concerning you, you will feel much more relaxed.

Story With a Moral

I once had to make an important digital conference call to people from three different continents, all very connected to the senior leaders of their company. The pressure was on me to make sure I presented well. My lighting had to be perfect, my digital camera focused. I needed to look good and feel good.

Before "show time," I wrote down what was worrying me the most. Of the items that were in my control, I felt very confident that I had done the best I could to make sure there were no issues. My knowledge of the company, the lighting, microphone, and camera were all top-notch.

For everything I wrote on my list that was not in my control, I said, "Okay, that's not my issue." I wrote everything down and then ripped up the paper right before the call. I felt great after throwing those bits of paper in the garbage. I was ready for the international digital conference and I performed extremely well. I was on my A-game and I felt great, much less worried than before.

Moral of the Story	*Write down your worries, then throw them out. You **will** feel better!*

38. THE PERSON YOU SEE IS THE PERSON YOU WILL BE

What do all great actors and actresses do before they go on the stage? What do newscasters do before they take their seats in front of the camera? What do all great orators do before they step onto the stage to give a great presentation? They visualize. They visualize their success in their acting performance. They visualize their success and imagine looking into the eye of the camera. Prior to stepping into the limelight, they close their eyes and they meditate about what success looks like, sounds like, and feels like in order to be confident in communicating their message.

Before you begin your digital job interviews, I want you to visualize your success. Think about what it looks like and what it feels like. I want you to see the person you need to be during your digital job interviews—a professional, confident, and experienced applicant. You need to be at your best during your digital job interviews. Nothing but your best is acceptable in this current job market.

In my own career, before I go out on stage to do an executive presentation about my books, I visualize what success looks like. I think about what I need to do in order to connect on an emotional level with the audience that is in front of me. What I want you to do is take five minutes before your digital job interview begins and just relax, close your eyes, and visualize what you need to do in the next hour in order to get to the next level.

S tory With a Moral

I was once advising one of my vice presidents before a major presentation to a Fortune 500 company, and I asked him, "What do you see when you close your eyes before this presentation?" He said to me, "I see failure. I see people laughing at me as I fumble my words."

So I replied, "You cannot think like this. If you think like this, this is what you will become. You have to think positive and put yourself in the right frame of mind. Visualize your success!" We tried again to meditate to reduce his nerves, but unfortunately, it was too late. He already had it in his head that he was going to fail and he was too nervous to change his mind set. It was an utter mess. He could not present confidently, as everything he had visualized of failure was coming true.

Moral of the Story

Visualize your success so you can confidently bring it to fruition.

39. Time Zone

Where is the hiring party calling you from? Is he/she in a different state? A different country? The key question is really this: Is the hiring manager calling you from the same time zone? This is important to know so you can address the other person with the correct greeting—it might be 7 a.m. your time but 8 p.m. her time, in which case you need to say "Good evening" and not "Good morning." You need to be in sync with the hiring manager in terms of the time of day. Think about your background, too. Don't have your video camera focused outside your window with the sunshine pouring in when it's 8 o'clock at night for the other person. Think of your homemade broadcasting studio as having no sense of day or night. Make sure you do your research before being contacted by the hiring manager so you know where the person is calling from.

Story With a Moral

I once worked for a company that had a team in India. Often I would videoconference with them and I would say "Good morning," when it was late afternoon there. They would ask "How has your day been?" when this was the first thing I was doing that morning. This caused interruptions and confusion in the flow of our conversation. Don't let this happen to you on your digital interview.

Moral of the
Story

Perform in the right time zone and be in sync with the hiring manager.

40. SHOWSTOPPERS

On Broadway there is a saying that the show must go on. For your digital job interviews, I say the show only goes on when you are ready; if you are not ready, you have a showstopper. A showstopper is anything that prevents you from conducting your digital job interview in the most professional, creative, and optimal way, such that you are the most attractive candidate for the position you are trying to obtain.

A showstopper can be anything from having the measles to the fact that your Internet connection just went down. Any issue that you cannot fix or address prior to the interview is a showstopper. If this happens to you, you need to inform the organization and the hiring manager that you will be unavailable at the scheduled time but that you are open to being rescheduled. Believe me, you do not want to present yourself when you are not at your best. You have more to lose than you have to gain, especially if you are sick. If there is something wrong with your voice, strep throat, for example, it is best to reschedule. Even major musicians, bands, and singers who have sold out concerts at Madison Square Garden with thousands of people who have already purchased tickets planning to attend, cancel their performances for one of these showstoppers. It's not ideal, but it happens. They have to cancel because they know they can't perform at their best. So, if you do not look well, sound well, or feel well, or if you are having technical issues, you must recognize this showstopper and reschedule your digital interview.

You may be concerned that rescheduling your digital job interview makes you look bad, but it would be a whole lot worse if you tried to go through with it when you were not feeling your best. I highly recommend that you reschedule, get everything set up, and then perform at your best when you are ready. Just remember that it is now absolutely crucial that you are ready to rock-and-roll when the rescheduled interview takes place. At that time, you should apologize to the hiring manager and explain the unsolvable nature of your showstopper. Make this apology professional, simple, and to the point.

You also want to be aware that if you need to reschedule, let the other person and his/her organization know as soon as possible. The most valuable thing in a person's life, which cannot be replaced, is time. I hate to see people wasting their time, and even more, I hate it when people waste my time. So the minute you know you have a showstopper, you must notify the other party that you cannot attend the interview. This also opens up the door for rescheduling immediately. Let's say you've lost your voice. Take a sufficient amount of time to get better and then reschedule as soon as possible. This will show the company and the hiring manager that you are intelligent, responsible, and time-efficient, and that you have common sense. You are willing to admit you cannot perform at your best right now and understand the responsibility of respecting everyone's time and rescheduling as soon as you can. Demonstrating that you want to keep the ball rolling will prove that even when you are not at your best, you are still a professional.

Story With a Moral

I was once asked to have lunch with a candidate who was interested in working for my company. Two minutes prior to our scheduled meeting time, the person called to tell me we needed to reschedule. I was already on my way to meet her and was definitely not happy about this. It made this person look distracted, unorganized, and unprofessional. This was a waste of my time, and to top it all off, she did not even apologize; she merely asked when we could reschedule.

Moral of the Story *Don't be like this person. If you encounter a showstopper, let the other party know immediately. Reschedule the digital interview asap, and let the show go on.*

Part Two:

Conducting

41. Don't Miss Your Cue!

How would you feel if after paying $150 dollars to go to a concert in New York City, five minutes before the show was supposed to start you saw actresses running in, props still being set up, and no one ready to perform? You would probably feel disappointed and unimpressed. It's the same thing when you are conducting a digital interview. You must be ready to go well before "showtime." You need to be set up, organized, and mentally and physically ready. You can't just be hanging out, looking around your office or playing solitaire on your computer, and then suddenly the interviewer calls in and catches you looking unprepared and unprofessional.

You must be sitting in your "action position" in your chair at your neat and organized desk, waiting to start the interview. Even if the other person isn't ready, that's not really your concern. You can't control the other actors and actresses in a show; you can only control yourself. If the hiring manager isn't ready, don't let that impact your professionalism—be patient, kind, and humble. Make sure you're ready to conduct the interview, no matter what. Make sure that you look your best, that your sound and camera are ready, and that your lighting is perfect.

Be ready, be patient, be professional.

Story With a Moral
In my professional life, I often give lectures at universities and conferences. I begin preparing

for these lectures four days prior and arrive a few hours early to each event. On one such occasion I was unable to get to the event early and it was a complete disaster. Nothing worked—the projector didn't work, my laptop wouldn't connect, and I had no idea where to stand in order to be in the correct lighting. It was a mess.

| Moral of the Story | *Don't let this happen during your digital interviews. Don't get caught unprepared. Be ready early and remain professional. Don't let delays on the other end negatively impact you.* |

42. REMOVE ALL BARRIERS

Building a relationship in person is hard enough; try doing it during a time-allotted interview over the Web. In order to bond quickly with the person conducting the interview, you need to have a direct visual line to him/her. This means having nothing in front of you that would block the hiring manager's view of you. There shouldn't be any objects between you and the person on the other end of the camera. Your keyboard should not be in front of you; put aside your paper clip bowl and your rubber-band ball. Likewise, your microphone should be placed to the side. There should be nothing but a clear, unobstructed view of you and the hiring manager.

After years of graduate studies at Fordham University in New York, I have learned that any object placed between two people actually functions as an impediment or obstruction, psychologically speaking. It is like a roadblock that you have to circumvent before moving forward. Think about news anchors—do they have anything in front of them other than their notes? No, they know better than to have anything that might impede their message. The only items you may have in front of you are paper and a pen and a copy of your resume. These should be lying flat in front of you or be pushed to the side until you need them.

Story With a Moral

My siblings and I had to go to confession when we were in Catholic school. It was a bit spooky—being lined up by the nuns, having to think about all your sins, and then confessing them to the priest. As an 8 year old, going to the confessional booth and speaking through a dark black screen (for anonymity) made me feel scared and isolated. The only thing I could see was the silhouette of the priest listening to me and then telling me to stop fighting with my brother and sisters and to go say a few Hail Mary's and one Our Father, just in case. So being the good Catholic boy that I was, off I would go, but I did not feel any great connection with God or the priest, with whom I had not even made eye contact. There was a great barrier between us—that dark black screen.

The Catholic Church finally got smart and removed that screen. Now there are no obstructions. People going to confession can feel a sense of engagement and relief as they confess their sins, and they walk away feeling better than they did before.

Moral of the Story	*Do as the Catholics do—make sure there are no barriers present during your digital interviews. A clear line of sight makes for an accessible relationship.*

43. STORYLINE

What is the theme of your digital job interview? Is it going to be a drama? A horror movie? A love story? A mystery? A tragicomedy? My suggestion is that you make it an action movie. Put your life into action. Share with the hiring manager what you have done, what you can do, and how you can help solve the company's problems.

Before I go see a movie, I make sure I know what kind of movie it's going to be. I am not really interested in horror movies or romantic comedies. Sure, they're fine to watch at home on the couch with my wife, but if I am paying good money to go out to the theater, I want *my* kind of movie. I want an action film with a strong plot and a great storyline, something that keeps my brain active and engaged. Similarly, you need to make sure you have the right storyline prepared when you go into your digital job interviews. You need a theme that encompasses who you are and what you do. Most managers hire people because they are going to fit into the job. You need to explain how you will take action to make the organization better, more profitable, and more successful.

I would highly recommend that you frame your narrative—what you plan on telling the hiring manager—as an action story. Most hiring managers want to hear your ideas on two key issues: how you will make them money, and how you will save them money. How are you going to drive up revenue and save this company money? In order to do this, you need to be a person of action. Companies pay for action. They pay for people who can execute. If your storyline is a horror story, you may keep your interviewers on the edge of their seats, but they may also end up having nightmares about you in their office. If your storyline is a love story, you may make your interviewer like you, but that isn't all you need to get to the next step. First and foremost, you need to be a person of action. Use the right storyline to get the hiring manager to fall in love with you for the right reasons—namely, that you will be a great fit and further the success of the company.

It should go without saying your digital job interview should not become a fictional storyline. I don't mean fictional as in made-up (although of course you do not want to invent facts or lie on your interview); rather, I mean fictional as in things that could have happened but didn't. Don't talk about how you *could* have changed your previous company or how you *could* have created a strong communication system. You want to talk about events that happened, what you actually did. Don't spend all your time talking about your past; rather, use your past to tell your interviewer what you can do today, based on your previous success. How does your past experience translate into value for this company in the future? That will be interesting for them to hear and (hopefully) inspire them to hire you.

I want you to start thinking about what your storyline is before your digital job interviews. What is the theme, and how are you going to carry it throughout the duration of your interview? Everyone loves action in Hollywood. Some of the top-grossing movies of all time are action movies—*Spiderman*, *Die Hard*, *Mission: Impossible*, *Independence Day*. These action-packed movies keep people on the edge of their seats, cheering for the heroes. You need to be that hero. You need to be the candidate who makes the interviewer say, "We need you, we want you, and we are going to pay you what you're worth because you're going to help change our organization for the better." That's what it's all about—changing the organization for the better. For this, companies are willing to pay you a lot of money. Make sure you have it straight in your head in terms of what you are planning to say during your interview and how you are planning to present the storyline. Before you turn on your Webcam and microphone, I want you to think about what the storyline is, the theme that you will use to frame what you say during your interview.

Think about your three top actions. For example, you can say you are a problem solver and explain exactly how you solve those problems. We all know that everyone, including organizations as a whole, has problems. Your value to this company will be determined in terms of the action you can take. What you actually did in the past to help an organization become more profitable and how you can apply that action to this new company in your new role. These are some of the key things you want to start thinking about and then incorporate into your storyline during your digital job interviews. Make sure you build up to the action lines in the first few minutes. If you've seen *Superman*, you know that it doesn't start with him saving the world. There is build-up that provides the necessary background for his character. Give yourself some build up in your digital interview. Give the person the facts about who you are, what you can do, and then hit him or her with the "wow factor" of what you've done in the past and how you can do this for the new company in the future.

There is a huge need everywhere for people who can lead, those who can make the world a better place. Your digital job interviews need to be filled with the actions that prove you are one of these people. Use action words strategically during your digital job interview. Make your stories action-packed. Make it exciting, make it interesting, and make sure the hiring manager is sitting on the edge of his or her seat, enraptured by your story.

Story With a Moral

My daughter, Kaitlyn, is a wonderful writer. She has such a powerful imagination that when I read her papers that come back from her teacher, I am just blown away. They are colorful and action-packed, with vivid word choices. The way she develops her stories is just outstanding. You absolutely have to read through to the end to find out what happens!

Moral of the Story	*Fill your storyline with action so that the hiring manager will take action and offer you the job.*

44. COMMERCIALS

When you think of a digital interview, you wouldn't necessarily think that there would be any commercials; but there actually are. These are not your normal commercials, obviously—breaking away from your scheduled programming to bring you a 60-second pitch of why you absolutely have to have this particular brand of laundry detergent. Rather, they are subtle sound bytes that resonate throughout your digital interview.

Think about the qualities or skills you want your interviewer to associate with you—for example, leadership, innovation, or creativity. These are the characteristics you want to "advertise" in your "commercials." These terms should be repeated several times throughout the interview. *You* are the product being promoted in these commercials.

After you answer one question, provide a short summary at the end. Your summary is like a commercial—a concise advertisement of your strengths that pertain to the question. By including these short statements several times during your interview, you will create a strong, positive image of yourself in the interviewer's mind.

Story With a Moral
No one likes commercial interruptions during their favorite television show. You must make your "commercial" short and enjoyable. Think about your favorite commercial and why you

like it—I enjoy the GEICO auto insurance ads in which talking animals promote their services. These commercials are simple to understand and enjoyable to watch. Promote your own characteristics in a similar manner during your digital interviews.

Moral of the Story	*Let subtle sound bytes pepper your interviews to remind hiring managers of your strongest traits.*

45. Make Your Interviewer Feel Like a Million Bucks

How do you feel when someone helps you out when you are down? When a partner at works gives you the heads up that your boss is in a bad mood and now is not the time to ask for a raise? You most likely say, "Thanks for helping me out and looking out for me." Similarly, during your digital interviews, you want to make your interviewer look good and feel good. Maybe your interviewer is nervous because he or she does not have a lot of experience with digital interviewing. Maybe his or her camera is out of focus. Lend a helping hand where you can to help the interviewer look good during the interview. At this moment you are a good person doing the right thing and making yourself look good in the process.

If you see the interviewer breaking a sweat or getting frazzled, make sure you turn the situation around onto yourself. You might say, "Digital interviews sometimes make me nervous. I always prefer face-to-face." This allows you to connect on a more human level. Say something nice (and mean it!) to the person interviewing you: "I really like that tie" or "That looks like a very nice office." Try to compliment the person on the other end of the camera; it will go a long way toward breaking the ice.

If you can't hear your interviewer, ask him to get closer to the microphone or increase the volume. Think of yourself as the stagehand for the interviewer, enabling him to sound great so you can hear him on the other end.

Story With a Moral

Once I was conducting an international interview for an executive-level opportunity. I was all set up from my end to start the digital interview, but the person on the other end was just sitting there, visibly nervous, his shirt soaked with sweat. I said, "Are you okay? Don't worry—I don't bite. I am not a TV producer looking to cut your show. I just want to talk with you to see if it's a good fit here for our company." The poor guy was so happy to just relax. His body looked less tense and he appeared to stop sweating. He was relaxed and able to proceed with the interview.

By making your interviewer feel good...you feel good.

By making your interviewer sound good... you sound good.

Moral of the Story	*Being helpful during your interview proves you can be helpful in the office. There is a direct correlation between doing the right thing and getting a reward for it!*

46. Talk *to* Them, Not *at* Them

It is sometimes difficult not to talk *at* a person, especially when you are speaking into a microphone and looking at the other person on a screen. You must remember that you are talking to a living, breathing person just like you on the other end. The key to talking *to* a person and not *at* a person is engaging the other person in what you are saying during your digital interview.

Don't think of it as throwing words and ideas at the screen, hoping the interviewer will reach out and grab them. It's like my MBA students at Sacred Heart University: When I am asking them engaging questions and they get stuck, sometimes I can see their minds going to the dark side—*What wild ideas can I throw at Professor Bailo to get me off the hook?* Well, it never works, and I often just hear a jumble of words being flung at me. Don't talk *at* your interviewer like this; it adds no value to the interaction. Engagement is the key. Read the reactions on the other person's face as you speak. Do they seem connected? If not, you are talking *at* them and not *to* them.

I was watching a show on The History Channel the other day, in which a business owner was trying to get a new line of men's suits into a major, high-end retail store. His strategy was to talk to a reporter of a major design magazine to showcase his new designs, hopefully grabbing retail's attention in the process. He somehow managed to get the magazine reporter into his offices, and off went the business owner, talking, talking, talking *at* the reporter, instead of *to* the reporter. You could tell by the reporter's facial expression that he was getting upset and probably thinking that he was wasting his time. The owner/ designer did not understand that he needed to talk *to* the reporter to create engagement, and, predictably, the meeting went horribly wrong. Not a good way to connect with people!

S tory With a Moral

My son, Connor, is an All-Star baseball player. When I practice with him in our backyard, sometimes I am nervous he is going to hurt me if he throws the ball *at* me. A fast ball wildly pitched at me could take my head off! It is only when he throws the ball *to* me, making sure I am connected with him before the ball leaves his hand, that I can catch it and throw it back to him.

Moral of the Story

Don't throw words and thoughts at your interviews. Share creative, interesting thoughts and ideas all weaved together with the inter- viewer. Don't hit him on the head; instead, make a connection by talking to him, not at him.

47. Eye Direction

I want you to think of your eyeballs as a compass. Wherever your eyes go, the hiring manager's eyes will follow. When I was a kid walking around New York City, I would often just stand on a corner, looking up at the skyscrapers. People walking by would also look up, wondering what I was so fascinated with. I bet you've done this yourself, whether it's following someone's gaze up in the sky or rubbernecking on the highway at an accident in the oncoming lane. The same holds true for your digital job interviews. If you are not looking straight ahead at the other person, you are essentially redirecting the interviewer's gaze away from you and the task at hand. Your eyes will direct the other person's to whatever focal point you choose. The only focal point you want him to have is your face, as you describe why you are a great candidate for the position. If the hiring manager is looking at you, focused on your face, there is a greater probability that he'll connect with you on an emotional level over the Web, thereby getting a better sense of who you are. This is such a small step but a very important one. If you are shifting your eyes around and not looking directly at the other person, it shows a lack of confidence and distracts from the content of your interview. Don't allow your hiring manager to lose focus or direction.

Story With a Moral

My executive friend had just purchased a new digital watch before a video conference call. He was so excited about it and was constantly playing with the different settings, like a kid at a candy store. During the team videoconference, whenever you looked at his image on the screen, his eyes were on his watch. He wasn't holding his watch in front of his face, but glancing down at his wrist under the table. This gave the impression that he was inattentive and self-centered. He didn't seem focused on the discussion and, as a result, no one was focused on what he had to contribute.

Moral of the Story	*Stay focused on the interviewer, and focus on your path to a new career.*

48. SHARE THE SPOTLIGHT

Some people really like to be in the spotlight and the center of attention. Movie stars, Broadway actors and actresses, even high school theater company performers love it when the big, bright lights shine on them. I want to make sure you understand that it takes two stars to make a great digital interview. Sometimes you are the star actor, other times you are the director or the costume designer. The role I want you to play is the action hero. Be a more professional, creative, innovative, better-spoken, better-looking version of James Bond. Think about how a James Bond movie works. He always has a main supporting character. They share the spotlight together to team up and defeat the bad guy. At the end of the movie, the viewer loves both Bond and his sidekick.

During your digital job interview, you need to share the spotlight with the hiring manager. It is not all about you and your background and what you can do. Make eye contact with the hiring manager and give her the correct social cues through your video camera. You must give her the opportunity to speak, to be heard, and to be understood. This way, you can assess her accurately in order to connect with her and drive the action home. In order to be selected for a face-to-face interview, you need to understand that sometimes the spotlight will be on the hiring manager. You need to collaborate, just as they do in the James Bond movies. It's difficult to have a successful movie or Broadway show with only one star. Most audiences appreciate it when the main actor shares the spotlight. Likewise, during your digital job interview, share the attention. Listen to all the great things the hiring manager has done, and then tell her your positive thoughts about these goals and accomplishments. Make sure you are excited for the right reasons—in other words, don't shamelessly stroke the hiring manager's ego just to get the job. Be sincerely engaged and happy to hear what the other person has to say. When you turn the spotlight on the other person, it actually serves to highlight more of your own key assets. This shows you are intelligent and insightful, and aware that people working together is what makes success.

The same thing applies when you are speaking with multiple people on your digital interview. In this situation, imagine a spotlight moving around the table. The executive vice president of technology may be asking you questions that you can answer by also engaging the president of the company. Don't allow yourself to become distracted and forget whom you are speaking to. You need to give your full attention to whomever is in the spotlight. Then, in your response, you can move the spotlight to another person, keeping everyone engaged in the conversation. Don't think of this as a break in the interview; the game is still on! Just because you are not in the limelight does not mean you are not part of the interview. That hiring manager is looking at you and thinking, *Is this candidate eager to engage in the conversation? Is this candidate listening to each of us? Is he or she really understanding?* Don't ever let your guard down, because that spotlight can easily be shifted right back to you. Don't think you can hide the shadows and disengage. Give every person taking part in the digital interview the necessary attention in a professional, courteous way, just as a star on Broadway gives the spotlight to each character as they speak or sing their part.

Story With a Moral

When I am teaching an MBA class in leadership, I try to put the spotlight on each one of my students. I may call out someone randomly and then, after his response, ask him to select someone else in the class who can answer the next question. This forces everyone to be on their toes at all times—you never know when you are going to be called upon to answer questions in my class! My students have to really pay attention. I expect everyone to know about or have some opinion on whatever I ask them. This learning tool keeps everyone fully engaged and on the edge of their seats. The spotlight goes around to different students and then back to me for an all-inclusive learning experience.

Moral of the Story   *Share the spotlight, share the credit, share the success.*

49. Pay Attention to Time

During your digital interview, time is on your side, but you must be sure to use your time wisely. It can never be replaced, purchased, or exchanged. It is finite. It is of limited supply, so you *must* maximize the time you have during each of your digital interviews.

In my research I've found that having a clock hanging on the wall behind the camera works well. This will allow you to monitor your time in a subtle way: you can quickly glance up and know how much time you have left and where you are in the interview. (Just make sure you choose a clock that doesn't make any noise. You don't want something that sounds like an egg timer distracting you during the interview.) Never look at your watch during an interview! This is rude and unprofessional. It suggests you are thinking about other things you need to do and places you need to be; to the interviewer, you're not making the digital interview your number-one priority. This will cause the hiring manager to question your candidacy for the position.

Before you create your storyline, consider the amount of time you have for your digital interview. Just as every television show has a schedule of events, so must your interview. In your case, you have the introduction, the body, and the conclusion. The high points of the interview should be in the body of the interview. You don't want to spend a ton of time on the greeting or introduction and not have enough time to express why you are the best candidate for the position and how powerful your credentials are in terms of helping the hiring organization.

Note: Even though you have a clock you can refer to behind the camera, you should still wear a watch during your interviews. Buy a professional-looking, high-quality watch: no themed watches, please. Wear a timepiece that enhances your professional image.

Story With a Moral

One year ago, I was interviewing an executive for a chief marketing officer role. I was in Connecticut and the candidate was in Mexico. The candidate came highly recommended, was highly educated and extremely experienced professionally, and seemed to have all the right stuff for the job. The digital interview started off well, but the candidate couldn't seem to get out of first gear. He seemed excited to be talking to me about everything but this specific job. He explained his background and previous responsibilities, all of which fit perfectly for this position, but the fact that he spent so much time talking about his past told me that he had trouble managing his time well. If he couldn't manage his time during his digital job interview, how could I ever expect him to manage his time in the office?

Moral of the Story	*Keep track of the time and use it wisely, with focus and purpose; prove you are worth the interviewer's time.*

50. Don't Forget You're on the Air

From one hour before your digital interview to 15 minutes afterward, you must be in the zone. During this critical time period, do not let your guard down! Remember, the camera is always on, so the hiring manager will probably see everything you do. Do not use the camera as a mirror to admire your reflection or fix your hair. Be in the zone and on your A-game at all times. Nothing else matters than acing this digital interview.

Additionally, consider the fact that there may be a slight delay in the image and sound transmission, in which case you'll need to account for it by moving a bit more slowly and enunciating your words distinctly. You may want to practice this beforehand to make sure you're not over- or underestimating the delay.

Story With a Moral

Last week I attended my daughter's talent show. It was an array of second- to eighth-graders entertaining the community with their instruments, dances, gymnastics, and singing. My daughter worked extremely hard, practicing every day on her viola for this day. I was amazed at how cute they all looked, but how woefully unprepared they were once they were on stage. It seemed like they were never told that everything they did on stage—from scratching their heads to talking to their friends—would be seen by hundreds of people in the audience. They did not realize they were on the air, live in real time, and this distracted from the talent they were displaying.

Moral of the Story	*Remember that everything—everything—you do when you're "on the air" during your digital job interviews is going to be watched, judged, and interpreted, either negatively or positively.*

51. Pilot Episode

I always love watching the new shows that come out every season. There are so many genres to chose from—action, police, drama, documentary, comedy, and reality TV. Each season typically starts out with about 30 new shows, but after the broadcasters tabulate the number of viewers for each, the number of shows drops to only one or two. It seems that the networks are always looking for the next new, exciting pilot to test. The success of the pilot will determine whether the company wants to sink a lot of time and money into continuing the show.

Your digital job interview is your pilot episode. If you can look and sound professional over the Web, you may be allowed to proceed to prime time. Just like that network show that wants to be on at the ideal time, when most people watch TV, you want to get the prime time spot at this company. Go into your digital interview with the mindset that this is your pilot episode. You want to be picked up by that major TV station or cable network and have a long-running show. To do this, you must be that new, exciting episode; *you* must be that new person offering new insights, new concepts, new ideas to this organization.

Hiring managers will also want to know if you will fit into the "theme" of their company. For example, think of the Discovery Channel: for this station, the main focus is educational (science and history), so the shows they are looking for must fit into those categories. Likewise, for your digital job interviews, you'll want to make sure that your pilot episode is crafted with the appropriate theme and audience in mind. Find the people who are most likely to purchase your pilot episode—meaning, of course, you need to find the company that is most likely to value your skill set. Broadcast your pilot episode to the company where you can have a long-running, prosperous career.

Story With a Moral

Sometimes you take chances on things you are just not sure about. I recall a digital job interview I once had for a director position. I was located on the East Coast and the position was located in Texas. It was truly a blind pilot. I did not have the qualifications they were looking for, nor did I have the professional background required, but they felt I had the right attitude, mindset, and educational background to at least be interviewed. Everything went smoothly as we Skyped—I was well-prepared, I had done my research, I had the proper equipment, and I ran everything according to my script. But even though my performance was excellent, they didn't sign me for the long run because I was not a good fit for the position.

I didn't give up. Right after that interview I tested my "pilot" with the right "channel" (the right organization). This time my pilot was purchased; the right company offered me the face-to-face interview and, eventually, the position.

Moral of the Story	*Market yourself to the right organization to land the long-running position that will bring success to you and your new company.*

52. Don't Be a Flop

In the movie business, there are some movies that are both critically acclaimed and huge successes. Think of the award-winning *Argo* and *Life of Pi*. On the opposite side of the spectrum, there are movies that are terrible flops, both critically and monetarily— movies that cost millions of dollars to produce that no one has ever heard of. I don't want your digital job interview to be a flop! In order to ensure that your digital job interview is a great success, make sure you are well-prepared on all levels: physically, mentally, emotionally, and technologically.

What do Broadway actors and actresses have to say as to why some of their performances are better than others? Go stand in the alley outside the stage door and ask them yourself; they will tell you it is all about *preparation*. Those short-lived productions that no one has ever heard of didn't enjoy a long run most likely because the key players were unprepared. Don't let your digital interview become one such short-lived spectacle. If you prepare well enough and you are ready and willing to do a stellar job, your performance will be great. On the other hand, if you fail to prepare— if you choose not to do your homework (reading this book, getting the right lighting, spending a little money to conduct a professional interview)—then your performance may very well be a complete flop.

Now, if you do have the misfortune of having a digital interview that turns out to be a flop, I don't want you to be negatively impacted. Turn it into a learning experience—how can you improve next time? It is inevitable that you will encounter problems and issues that will be relatively easy to fix. You may need to spend a little more money to improve your equipment, or you may have to spend a little more time practicing your introduction or conclusion. But the point is, it is possible to improve. So if your digital interview is a flop, take a deep breath, acknowledge that it was not an award-winning interview, figure out why, and then make sure it never happens again.

I know from personal experience that my greatest growth, both personally and professionally, has come from making mistakes. It's like Shakespeare's plays (which have certainly proved to be long-running)—the greatest growth of the primary players usually comes from tragedy. You learn and you grow. So don't be discouraged, and don't stop trying. Evaluate your flop; dissect it in order to understand what went wrong and what caused you to flop in the first place.

After a serious gaffe, it's okay to laugh at yourself and think, *I can't believe I did that!* We're all human; we all make mistakes. Maybe you forgot to turn on the sound. Or maybe you started speaking into the microphone and found you could hear yourself in the interviewer's speakers. Do not give up. Do not shut down and say you'll never be able to master the digital interview. Do not let these negative thoughts into your mind. Just laugh it off, learn from it, and move on.

There is not one contact in my LinkedIn account whose life has worked out perfectly. It just doesn't happen like that. The most successful people I know are the ones who fell on their face and then got up and kept going. Some of my professional friends suffered flop after flop in their interviews, but they kept learning from their errors and just got better and better.

Story With a Moral

Once I was creating an online video for educational purposes and I was completely unprepared. I wasn't comfortable with the camera or the stage, and the heat from the lights kept making me sweat profusely. It was a complete and utter flop. It was a waste of money and equipment, but not a waste of time. I learned if I do not fully prepare, I will not have an award-winning performance. If I want to create a great video, I have to do my homework and make sure I am ready to be successful. If I, or you, have the wrong mindset going into a video production, it will be a flop.

Even big-name stars have been in flops. I'm sure you can think of a time when you were watching some movie that went straight to video and thinking, about the lead actor, *That guy looks familiar,* only to realize that he was a major motion-picture star making millions a week, yet there he was in that terrible movie! Don't think that one flop means always a flop. Everyone starts somewhere. Make sure you learn from your mistakes so you can make it to the big time.

Moral of the Story
Learn from your mistakes, practice, and become a long-running success.

53. No Special Effects

I always love watching action movies. The special effects create an unbelievable cinematic adventure. The acting usually isn't superb, and these movies usually don't win any awards on their own, but the special effects are what make them such huge hits. The focus is not the actors, but the special effects. Cars blowing up, helicopters crashing to the ground, human skin being peeled away from the body—all exciting and even shocking spectacles. In this kind of movie, what do people talk about after the show? The special effects.

What do you want your interviewer to remember and talk about after your interview? Do you want her to talk about the different sound and lighting effects? No, you want her to remember you. You, and nothing else; *you* need to be the center of attention on your digital interview. No explosions, no high-tech bells and whistles—just human-to-human connection.

Story With a Moral

Once I was sitting in an executive presentation in which the presenter was using PowerPoint slides. At each change in slide there was an audio clip—*whoosh! zoom! pop!* Then information would fly in from different directions onto the colorfully decorated slide. After the first few slides everyone was anticipating what special effect would happen next, but no one heard a word the presenter said. Everyone was intrigued by how well the slides were put together, how cool it looked with all the fancy-schmancy effects, but the reality of it is that the special effects distorted and even blocked the message. The message wasn't conveyed and, in the end, the presenter wasted his time.

Don't let special effects take over your ability to interview well. Do not distract the interviewer from who you are and what you have to offer for the position.

| Moral of the Story | *Be your own special effect in your digital interview: create a memorable impression with your skills.* |

54. Grandma's Rocker

You shouldn't be moving around a lot during your digital job interviews. If you get nervous, take a deep breath and try to relax. Don't rock back and forth in your office chair as though you were in grandma's rocker. If you are sitting in a swivel chair, don't move back and forth, as tempting as that may be. You should be facing forward and looking the hiring manager in the eyes. This conveys confidence, intelligence, and professionalism. There is no need to be rocking or moving around. This is not a warm summer night on the porch, sitting in grandma's rocker—this is a professional digital interview. If possible, make sure your chair is locked in place so you won't be tempted to move around. Also, keep your hands still on the desk in front of you.

Story With a Moral

I can remember being at a board meeting when people sitting around the table were rocking back and forth while one of the key executives was presenting on finance or marketing. Some people were nervously tapping their pen against their hand. These movements were so distracting that I ended up missing part of the presentation.

Moral of the Story

Don't be a moving target and cause your interviewer to miss part of your presentation—be still and be successful.

55. Moves Like Jagger

I don't know about you, but I love dancing. It's always fun to get out on the dance floor and move around to the music with my wife and kids. Dancing lets you release all your pent-up energy and really enjoy life. Dancing is great, but you don't want to be busting a move like Mick Jagger during your interviews. Mick Jagger (or whatever world-famous rock or pop star you pay tons of money to see) is not the model you should emulate for your digital interviews. Just as you shouldn't be swaying or swiveling in your chair, you also shouldn't be bopping around, bouncing to music and jumping left and right. This would be a complete distraction, and, depending on your Internet connection, you could end up looking like one big blur. I don't think anyone wants to hire a person whose face they can't even see. What I want you to do is stay steady and focused. When you need to reach for a document, you must do so with a very calculated movement, not something resembling a free-style dance move. If you appear to be dancing around, you will look unprofessional. Save your "moves like Jagger" for when you are celebrating, *after* you get the job offer.

Story With a Moral

I recently went to my daughter's third-grade biography performance, in which all of the kids dress up as a famous historical figure and give a short report about him or her. My daughter decided to go as Laura Ingalls

Wilder, the woman who wrote *Little House on the Prairie*. She did an absolutely fantastic job, and I'm not just saying this because I'm her father. The reason she did so well was because she planted her feet and gave her presentation looking straight at the audience. She didn't bury her hands in her pockets or look around distractedly. She was focused and completely engaged. She engaged the audience and made eye contact with different people in the crowd. Other students stared fixedly only at their parents or kept switching their weight from one foot to the other. Of course I understand that these children are only nine years old and were nervous, but a strong presenter cannot be moving around like that.

The same principle applies to your digital interviews. You will have even more problems in your digital interviews than if you were moving around like that in a face-to-face presentation. Through the screen, you'll have sound and visual issues, and you'll give your interviewer a headache just from watching you. This will ruin your connection, literally and figuratively. If you look as though you have ants in your pants, you are going to come across as a nervous third-grader, not the professional, talented individual you are. Remember, maintain good eye contact, employ calculated movements, and keep your connection strong.

Moral of the Story	*Don't make the moves like Jagger; be composed, calm, and still to land your job interview.*

56. Make Love to the Camera

Do you ever wonder why some actors get $10 million for a movie while others only get union rates? Ever look at a fashion magazine and say, "Wow, what a great photo!" The image really connects you with that person. Did you ever look at a painting and actually feel the emotion in it? Did you ever feel as though you were part of a movie when, really, you were sitting on your couch eating popcorn in your pajamas? You become emotionally invested in the characters even though you knew it was just a movie. Why and how does this happen?

This happens because actors are professionals. They know how to transfer their emotions via the camera to the audience. You need to do the same during your digital interviews. You need to be able to communicate your feelings about the position and the company to the hiring manager through your Webcam. You have to learn to convey your humanity and emotions through a screen, as opposed to face-to-face. In order to do this, you need to be able to feel comfortable in front of a Webcam before you start giving digital job interviews. You have to be mentally, physically, and emotionally in the zone. Actors and actresses whom I have spoken with indicate that they don't think of the camera as a piece of technology; they think of it as a person with whom they are actually connecting. So don't think of your Webcam as a piece of machinery; think of the human being you will be connecting with using this technology.

More than just another human being, think of the other person as someone whom you love and care for. This way it will be easier to transfer human emotion through the camera. Talk to your family and friends on Skype to get used to connecting with other people via this medium. Then, when it comes time to talk to the hiring manager, relax and send emotions just as you have practiced. The Webcam needs to be an extension of you—who you are, what you stand for, and your professional background must all be translated through the camera, over the Internet, and to the person on the other side.

There is an option on Skype that allows you to record yourself. If you use Skype, do this in order to see how you look and sound. Engage in a mock interview with a friend and listen to it afterward. Do you feel any emotion? Do you feel connected to your friend and the conversation?

Story With a Moral

I remember being at a town hall for a major corporate event. There were cameras set up around the room in order for the executive to connect with about 10,000 people globally. What a disaster! I sat right in front, and I could see the poor guy sweating and mumbling. The people in the audience turned and looked at each other with questioning looks. Others just looked bored, as though they were thinking about what they needed to buy at the grocery store on the way home.

Don't be like this executive. Connect with your audience through the camera. If you don't like being on video, you may want to try to make a simple YouTube video. Have fun and create something easy and short that will help you get comfortable. Laugh at your own video afterward to feel at ease. Then, when it comes time for your digital interviews, you'll be ready to go.

Moral of the Story	*To get your interviewer to feel invested, show emotion through the screen!*

57. Don't Butter Your Popcorn

I love going to the movies with my wife. Before we go into the movie theater, we usually stopped at the concession stand and, after considering the licorice, always go for the popcorn. Then we douse it with butter (or butter-flavored oil), the worst thing for you, but it's movie night out, so we splurge for a special treat. The popcorn goes in between us at the theater and we try not to disturb the people next to us while reaching into the popcorn bowl. A little crunching is acceptable at the movies, but not during your digital job interviews. The focus of each interview is as much about the needs of the person interviewing you as it is about you. So it should go without saying that you shouldn't be feeding your face during any interview, no matter how hungry you are!

During your interview, there should be no food, snacks, candy, or gum to be had anywhere. Not even mints. (And certainly no greasy butter or popcorn.) All of these can impede your ability to speak clearly and compellingly. It is hard enough for a hiring manager to understand a candidate over the Web. If you do not have high-quality equipment and a decent Internet connection, you may already be at a disadvantage. Do not compromise your connection any further by having food, snacks, gum, or mints in your mouth while you are trying to speak.

Story With a Moral

I can remember when I was looking to hire a director for a position in a digital marketing company. I was interviewing for an East Coast position with a candidate who was located on the West Coast. We connected and agreed to the digital job interview. Everything was going fine until the candidate reached for a few sunflower seeds while I was explaining the job responsibilities. I could not follow my own thoughts, as I was forced to listen to this person crunch away on his snack. Even worse, every few seconds he would turn away to the side to spit out the shells! I was horrified by his antics. This was completely unacceptable, and I lost all interest in this job candidate.

Moral of the Story

As much as you may be looking forward to putting on a show, don't butter your popcorn for your interview. Avoid food and snacks so you can speak clearly and compellingly about the many ways you can help this organization and the hiring manager.

58. Understudy

Broadway has a position known as an understudy. If the lead actor or actress gets sick or has an emergency, there is someone there to take his or her place and perform the role that the lead worked so hard to obtain, but could no longer fulfill. During your digital job interviews, as you are "performing" over the Web, you need to realize that you, too, have an understudy. There is another candidate out there who wants the job just as badly as you do. If you're not careful, this person can take the job away from you. Do not be outperformed by your understudy. The reason you are reading this book is to improve and be the best performer possible. You don't want to hand over this job to anyone else. You don't want to lose; you want to win! "Winning" means getting the job offer you've worked so hard for. You've done all the prep work: you've bought a quality microphone, high-definition camera, backdrop, and lighting, and you've created your script and set up your broadcasting room. But none of this means that you have the job—yet. You know that the job is yours only when they send you an offer letter. Only then can you celebrate being the top candidate and taking the next step in your career.

The reason I'm telling you about understudies is that you must consider what sets you apart from the others. There are many other candidates out there who are eager to take your place. Being aware of these understudies, these other people who would displace you, will motivate and encourage you to compete and perform at a high level. Don't let your understudy step up and rob you of your position.

I cannot tell you how many times I have spoken to executives, professionals, and students who thought their interviews went so well over the Web that they were sure they were getting the job. Sure enough, they were called in for a face-to-face interview, but they made the fatal mistake of forgetting about the understudy. They thought they were the only game in town when, in reality, they were facing some stiff competition. I want you to make sure that you *never* let your guard down. The fact that you have an understudy who could quickly move into your spot should keep you on your toes. This fact will drive you to perform at your best during all of your digital interviews. I don't want someone to take *your* role away from you. Do not be outperformed by an understudy.

S tory With a Moral

My son, Connor, is a very good baseball player. He has played Little League All-Stars and is currently on our town's travel team. He loves baseball, not only because he is very good at it and understands the game strategy, but also because of the other people on his team who bring a lot to the table. They are a great group and, as of this writing, just started the playoffs to the state championship.

Connor played a major role in their quest at Diamond Nations in New Jersey. This is three days of intensive baseball. Unfortunately, after several innings, Connor felt pain in his left foot; it turned out to be a hairline fracture, which meant he was going to be out of commission for a few weeks. He was sidelined and a different boy was tapped to play his position. Connor didn't want to be overtaken by his "understudy," so instead of sitting on the bench feeling sorry for himself, he went to every practice and even participated in some batting and throwing with a boot on his leg. He was eager to regain his position on the team as opposed to sitting on the bench.

Moral of the Story	*As well as you do during your interview, your understudy can quickly replace you. Don't let your guard down, and remain focused on what sets you apart.*

59. Don't Get Cancelled

Imagine working for years developing a Broadway show—getting all the actors and actresses together, the production, the studio, the theater, the costumes, and the sets. It takes a lot of time—and funding. The ultimate goal is to keep the show going and not get cancelled. Broadway shows get cancelled all the time. You might see a billboard about a brand-new show in New York City and, the next thing you know, it's gone. It just didn't work out. This also happens all the time on TV. You see the pilot episode of a show, but then you decide not to watch the following episodes. You see the show pop up occasionally over the next year or two, never becoming a big hit, and then it disappears.

This also can happen during your digital job interview. It is a sort of mental "cancellation" wherein the hiring manager stops thinking about you as a candidate and is no longer tuned in to what you're saying. He or she can't wait to turn off the Webcam and meet the next candidate. This person is no longer invested in you or what you bring to the table. You can be cancelled at any point in your interview, just as a show can be cancelled after the pilot episode or halfway through the first season. The difference is that you don't know when you're actually being cancelled. Because there are no billboards involved, you can't necessarily know when your digital interview is no longer getting you to the next step.

In my research, I have learned that the initial visual contact is the most important time in a digital job interview. It is in those few seconds, when the hiring manager sees you and you see the hiring manager, that the digital chemistry is created. That is when this person (hopefully) thinks, *I like what I see. I feel that I am connecting with this person and I want to continue the conversation.* This is when you can stop the polite chit chat and go into a more detailed conversation in terms of your background and experience and how you can be of value to this organization. Again, be aware that you can be cancelled at any time during this conversation. There is no giant red flag waving that lets you know when this has happened, so you need to perform at your best throughout the entire interview. Don't think that just because you have passed the initial screening, you are past the point of cancellation.

Sometimes you can't help being cancelled. Sometimes there just isn't any digital chemistry between you and the hiring manager, and you both know that it won't work out. This may not be your fault. In order to keep this from happening, make sure you are telling the other person what he needs to hear. Be truthful, be humble, and be helpful in solving the company's problems. Do not rush into the conversation part of your digital job interview. Make sure you connect with the interviewer and show him you understand what he is trying to do.

Sometimes *you* can cancel the *interviewer*. You may reach a point in your conversation when you realize this position is just not the one for you. If this happens to you (and it most likely will, as not every position will be a good fit), don't make any indication of it; you should remain courteous and professional the entire time. You may be tempted to say something about your misgivings, that you're not feeling a connection with the hiring manager or enticed by the position. But my recommendation is to not rule out the position before you have the opportunity to meet the other people at the company and get a feel for the environment in person.

Story With a Moral

I was once called for a digital interview to be the head of technology and digital analytics for a very high-end financial services consulting company. I had spent many hours preparing and educating myself on the company, the position, the people, and the corporate culture. I had reached out to my executive network and obtained inside information on the personalities and the people whom I would be meeting with online. Someone mentioned that one of the hardest interviewers to get past would be the chief administrative officer. Well, to my chagrin, it was true. I was canceled in the first 30 seconds of the interview. Why? Because I was completely unprepared for how direct and harsh this interviewer would be. The first words out of his mouth were, "You are too smart and creative—why would you want to work in this company?" I was thrown off balance and instantly we did not click. I could see all my hours of work and preparation going down the drain. What I should have done was try to understand where the question was coming from. I should have considered whom I was talking to—this person was looking for someone to come in and fix the issues in their technology. He wanted to find someone who would not make the company executives look bad in the process. I should have been smarter to know that this was an ego-based question and not immediately felt all my time and energy deflating.

Moral of the Story	*Try not to get cancelled before you've even begun your performance. Understand whom you are talking to and where his or her questions are coming from to keep from being shut down.*

60. "To Be Continued"

When I was a kid I used to watch a show called *Happy Days*. My brother, my two sisters, my mom, and my dad would all gather around the TV to watch this sitcom about young teenagers living out their lives in the 1950s. Sometimes an episode would need more than the allotted half hour to solve all the drama, and so, at the end of the show, the words "To be continued" would flash across the screen. I would spend the whole week wondering how they were going to neatly wrap up everything that had happened.

Keep this in your mind that a digital interview is just one more step in the right direction; it is not the whole show. You must strive to move forward to get to the face-to-face interview. When your camera and microphone have been turned off, you want your hiring manager to still be thinking about your interview, turning your skills over in his or her head, and wanting to continue interviewing you for the opportunity at hand. I want you to think about what might cause a hiring manager to continue thinking about you. I want your interview to be almost like a cliffhanger, wherein the interviewer finds you so interesting that he or she can't wait to meet you in person. How do you do this?

Don't just *tell* them what you have done; *show* them by telling a story about who you are and what you have accomplished. Be the intriguing, accomplished candidate with tons of potential who will put your interviewer on the edge of her seat. Then she will want to continue the process by meeting you, instead of feeling forced. Connect with your interviewer in such a way that she is just as excited as you are about the next step, the face-to-face interview.

Story With a Moral

I once had a digital job interview with a major technology company in California when I was on the East Coast. I was interviewing with an executive vice president, a very senior person in the company, and I remember him saying at the end of the interview, "I can't wait to meet with you. You seem like a very interesting person, just from your background and your personality." This is the kind of eagerness you want to instill. This allows you to bridge the gap from the digital world to the real world. When the Webcam is turned off, you want the hiring manager to be thinking about you and the conversation you just had, feeling positive and enthusiastic about meeting you in person.

Moral of the Story

Think "to be continued" until you get the job offer.

61. BLOOPERS

Life is full of bloopers. It is just how life is—sometimes it works and sometimes it doesn't. During your digital job interviews you may have a number of these little mishaps. Maybe the lights go out because they are set to a motion sensor and you weren't moving often enough to keep them on. Or maybe you reach for something and knock your microphone over with a big crash. In my research, I found that it is usually best to simply acknowledge the gaffe, apologize for it, and move on. Don't make a big deal about your bloopers; simply say that you realize there was a mistake and then continue with the interview. Maybe there is a problem with the sound—your volume is too high or too low. Acknowledge and apologize by saying something like this: "I realize the sound was a bit too loud on my end. My apologies." Don't spend any more time belaboring the point.

The real blooper is when something relatively minor goes awry during your digital job interview and you spend the next hour talking about it. This is a distraction and will completely negate any value you might otherwise bring to the interview. No one will hire you if you can't get back on track after a blooper. No one wants to listen to someone turn a small mistake into a long, exhausting apology and explanation of what went wrong. Think about the blooper reel that is sometimes included with DVDs. This shows that the actors and actresses are human, that they make mistakes and laugh about them. Obviously you don't have the luxury of editing and cutting out any of your bloopers, but you can certainly benefit from them. Demonstrate that you are human—you understand that bloopers pop up, and that is okay. Prove you can remain on topic, continue the conversation, and keep up your professionalism.

Sometimes you can use a blooper in order to inject a little humor into the situation. If you show that you have a sense of humor and that you don't frazzle easily, a blooper can actually help you. It shows that you can roll with the punches and not become distracted. You can also use a blooper to your advantage if you can tie it into something. For instance, if there is an issue with the sound, you could point out how you think that communication is incredibly important to a successful company. You can use this blooper to tell your interviewer that you created a community system at your last position. You have just turned that blooper into an Academy Award. You used it to your advantage to showcase how your mind works and what you can bring to the organization.

Story With a Moral

I remember watching the short snippets of bloopers that came on after my favorite television shows when I was a kid. It was interesting to see the actors and actresses when they made a mistake and broke from character, often with a laugh or a shocked expression. It was funny and it made them feel more real to me, as though they were sitting in my living room laughing right along with me at their mistakes. Of course, your goal is to have no bloopers during your digital job interviews. The best way to minimize the possibility that they will happen is to practice—become more adept by reading this book, watching the news, watching *60 Minutes*, and observing how the professionals do it. The more you know and the more you practice, the fewer bloopers you will ultimately have.

Moral of the Story	*Try to avoid bloopers, but if you have one, spin it to your advantage.*

62. The Group Shot

The group shot, also known as the group videoconference call, is one of the most difficult video events to master. Why? Because there are numerous things going on simultaneously that could distract you and cause you to lose focus—exactly what you don't want to do. When you are meeting with more than one person, one of the main things you have to work on is eye contact. I want you to identify the top three people whom you would benefit from the most and give them the most attention. It is impossible to give everyone an equal amount of attention so give less attention to the individuals who do not have the power or authority to influence your end goal—getting the job.

You may want to draw a little diagram to keep to track of who is who so you can remember everyone's name, title, department, and role, and, most importantly, who has the most influence in terms of getting you the position. Remember, that each person will interpret your emotions, tone of voice, and words differently, so make sure you put into practice everything you learned in this book. Don't think you can slack off because there are more people involved; quite the opposite. More people means you have to be even more on top of your game because now there are several individuals interpreting what you say and do.

Be very careful of your mannerisms and the words you use. Use each person's first name when addressing him or her. Done judiciously, this will help you keep the conference call organized. There may be a facilitator present who controls the dialog and who gets to speak next; this will make it easier for you to direct your questions appropriately when it is your turn to speak. The worst-case scenario is if multiple people try to speak at the same time. Then it becomes even more important for you to use first names. Proving you can be clear and organized in your group interview proves you will be clear and organized in the position.

Before a group digital interview, set down the ground rules of who is controlling the AV and who is asking questions: Is there a lineup of speakers? Make sure people identify themselves by their first name, last name, title, and department. This will assist you in tailoring your questions to that specific person as opposed to addressing the group as a whole. In these kinds of interviews, you want to be as specific as possible and make sure your questions and responses are appropriate for the particular person to whom you are speaking. Even though you may have six people staring at you, you only want to be thinking of one person at a time. Stay focused so you always know who is speaking and from what perspective. As you can see, in a group videoconference, control and focus are the name of the game.

Story With a Moral

Whenever I am presenting to a graduating class of a major business school I identify what section of the audience I am going to focus on. I tell myself what section of the audience I am trying to connect with, and, most importantly, I try to figure out what they want and need to hear. I attempt to exert control and focus in my presentation. I always ask myself, *What are the needs of these people in the audience?* It is their needs, not my own, that I am attending to. When someone in the audience asks a question, I ask him or her to stand up and state their name and title. This allows me to connect with them and identify where they are coming from with their question. Think about this when conducting a group digital interview—control and focus will make you stand out as a strong, professional candidate, even in a crowded room.

Moral of the Story

Stay focused and organized to be the star of a group videoconference.

PART THREE:
CONCLUDING

63. THE LAST ACT

The last act in any Broadway show is the great finale. It's the culmination of all the scenes, music, and lines that came before. It's when the actors and actresses put on their last grand performance to garner as much praise as possible. That's exactly what you need to do during your digital job interviews. Pull all the threads together for the last act. Bring it all home in the grand finale so that you receive the applause and recognition you deserve. The hiring manager should be excited enough after your digital job interview to say, "You are the one we want." How do you make this happen?

First, make sure you have all your key points ready to summarize what you spoke about during the interview. Talk about what the hiring manager needs and how you are uniquely qualified to meet those needs, then make three key points that really sum up the underlying theme or narrative. In the last act of the show, no one wants to be reminded of the little things that happened—the joke the minor character told in Act Two, or why the little girl cried in Act Three. Rather, the actors and actresses want to get across the underlying theme—making it big from starting at the bottom, or turning a frog into a handsome prince and living happily ever after. That is what you have to do in the last act—highlight the major theme. Once the Q&A is over and you see that you have only 10 minutes left, get ready for your last act. How do your background, education, and professional experience fit in terms of what the organization and the hiring manager are seeking? These three key points are what you need in order to wrap up your digital interview.

After you reiterate your key points, I want you to take the following three steps to conclude your last act:

1. First, thank the hiring manager for her time. There is no greater gift that a person can give you than her time. Time is the only item in the world that cannot be replaced, and everyone has a limited amount of it. So look into the hiring manager's eyes (not in a creepy way!) and truly thank her for her time and the consideration she has given you during the interview. This has been a great opportunity for you, and you want to make sure the other person knows that you know that.

2. Next, ask about the next steps. Now that you've spent an hour on the Web getting to know this individual, sharing your experiences, emotionally connecting, and making your case for how you can solve the company's problems, what happens next? My research has shown that if the person quickly responds, "I want to see you next week," that's an extremely good sign. A face-to-face interview is the next logical step if you're in the running, and that is exactly where you want to be headed as your digital interview comes to a close.

3. Finally, *tell her you want the job and why*. Tell her this is exactly what you have been looking for—precisely the type of work you

are experienced and interested in—and exactly how you can help them solve their problems. Just like the last act of a Broadway show, you want to be emotionally connected and confident in your performance. Just as audience members often hum the music from the last act on their way out the door, you want your interviewer to be singing your tune to the other executives at her company.

Story With a Moral

I can remember interviewing a candidate for an executive vice president position over the Web. The person was in California and I was in Connecticut. He looked good, was well-prepared, and had great qualifications. The digital interview went very well until it came to the last act. It just ended. It was like reading a book and discovering you're missing the last five pages, or watching a crime show and, just when they are about to announce who did it, the television cuts out. There was no wrap up, no conclusion, no key points that summarized his theme or story. I was completely shocked that this person, who appeared so professional otherwise, had no idea how to conduct the last act or that it was even important. I left my desk after the interview thinking about what was next on my daily agenda; I certainly wasn't singing the tune of this interviewee.

Moral of the Story | *Have the audience standing on their feet after your last act.*

64. Sign the Playbill

You just conducted your digital job interview and everything went great. Just as we were hoping, you looked and sounded professional, intelligent, and well-prepared, and you connected emotionally with the interviewer. Next, you get the call to come in for the face-to-face interview. Now comes the step that I call "signing the playbill." Have you ever gone to a Broadway show and then waited outside the stage door after the performance to try to get your favorite actor or actress to sign your playbill? He or she comes out smiling, maybe still wearing a costume, and signs your book with a smile. This is still all part of the show. If he or she came out angry and unfriendly, would you want to see another show that this individual is in? Chances are, probably not. The same thing goes for your digital job interview. Just because you got the face-to-face interview does not mean the show is over. It certainly doesn't mean you should let your guard down and stop looking for other jobs. It just means you are ready for the next step in this particular position. You should be very proud of yourself that you made it through the digital job interview with flying colors. Your hard work has paid off, just as it does for those hardworking Broadway actors and actresses when their show gets great reviews. However, they don't stop rehearsing once they get a standing ovation, and neither should you. Only when you receive that offer in writing can you say you have officially succeeded. Even then, you cannot stop signing your playbill. The networking that you do during your job interview and as you transition into your new career can take you to unforeseen heights in your professional life. Don't forget all the important things you learned during your digital job interview. Remember how you learned to communicate by connecting over the Web to continue to increase your professional contacts.

After your digital job interview and your confirmation of the face-to-face interview, I want you to continue to hone your interviewing skills. Even when you go for the face-to-face interview, it does not necessarily mean you'll get the job. You never know who else is competing for it. The ultimate goal is to get to know the company and the hiring manager, and land that job. There are still a lot of variables at play, so I want you to keep working on your general interviewing skills. Keep sending out your resume until you find a job that you love that meets all your needs and requirements. Keep signing your playbill, even after your digital interview success.

Story With a Moral

It is always exciting to be offered a new position. It validates who you are, what you are, and what you want to become in life. These months of hard work—finding a job opening, getting through your phone interview, your digital interview, the face-to-face interview to finally getting the offer—is like winning the gold at the Olympics. It is a wonderful feeling of accomplishment.

In my research I was amazed to learn how many people have been conducting digital job interviews, been offered the positions, and six months later, are back on the hunt for a new position. I think the problem is that, in these times of drastic change, one has to always be looking to "sign the playbill." You always have to be looking out for yourself and your next opportunity. You never know where it is going to come from. It can come from a friend, a discussion with a co-worker, or even the stranger sitting next to you on the train. It could come from something you read in the newspaper or see on the Internet. You always have to have your feelers out for your next playbill to sign. Look for your next opportunity to impress someone and continue growing as an individual. This can be applied to growth within your new career or growth toward a different job, but it is all about continuing to make those connections.

Moral of the Story	*Continue to sign your playbill and continue leaving your mark on the world.*

65. Roll the Credits

We all have someone who is invested in our success. Spouses, parents, siblings, grandparents, teachers, professors, priests, rabbis—at some point in our lives we have all been influenced by at least some of these people, and they deserve a bit of credit for our success.

You also need to share the credit with the people who helped with your digital job interviewing. If you took my advice, you already have some allies in the new organization, people who were willing to set up everything prior to the interview so you could test out all your equipment. In addition, there are administrative people who handled the scheduling and the meetings that made your digital job interview happen. At the conclusion of your digital job interview with the hiring manager, I want you to thank all of these people and make the hiring manager aware of what everyone has done to make the interview run smoothly. For example, you can say something like, "I just want to let you know I greatly appreciate Mary Sue's assistance in setting up this interview. She was kind enough to make sure everything was set up and working perfectly, and I would like to extend her some credit for that." You should also send everyone at the new company who helped you an e-mail or thank-you card to express your gratitude. They may not be the ones who make the final decision on whether or not you get hired, but genuine expressions of thanks go a long way.

Giving credit to these people will make both you and them look good to the hiring manager. This shows that you know you can't do it alone. No one can build success completely on his or her own. Sharing the credit proves you are not selfish or egotistical. This will make you look professional and honest, creating a positive connotation associated with your name during the entire hiring process.

Story With a Moral

Early in my career I was working for a senior vice president at Citibank. We had a major event going on during which we were tasked to present to an EVP on one of the major company initiatives. My team and I worked three weeks straight to acquire all the information and make sure it was accurately prepared for the EVP to look good at the presentation. Sadly, my staff and I watched the presentation conclude without any acknowledgment for our three weeks of hard work. That hurt. Don't do this. Know that giving credit where credit is due is a good thing. It shows you recognize the hard work other people do for you and acknowledge their success.

Moral of the Story	*Giving credit to others proves your own good credit.*

66. Wait Five Minutes Before Shutting Down

Congratulations! You made it through your digital interview. You went through all the preparation—reading this book, researching the company, purchasing and testing your microphone and camera, and setting up your studio. You conducted the interview with strong eye contact, engaging conversation, and a genuine emotional connection through the screen. You have completed your conclusion—giving credit where credit is due and initiating the steps to continue your conversation in person. Now all you have to do is finish. Let the hiring manager shut down his computer first; then, wait five minutes to be sure the other end is completely disconnected before you shut down your equipment. And finally, I would like you to do a debriefing.

Don't rush off the set. Don't let the last thing the hiring manager see be your hand already reaching to shut off your camera. Slow down. Once the hiring manager has shut down, spend five minutes thinking about what worked and what didn't during the interview. Obviously, don't say this out loud—you don't want the interviewer hearing you say "I don't think he liked me" right before he or she disconnects the sound. Don't throw away your interview at the last minute! Remember: calm, slow, and thoughtful.

Story With a Moral

I remember watching the Channel 7 news when I lived in Queens, New York, and learning everything that had happened during the day. I distinctly remember one broadcast, when the news reporter was reporting on a car accident in midtown Manhattan. She had completed the story and thought the cameras were off, and she actually flipped a crewmember the bird! Can you imagine? A news show broadcasted to millions of people, and this professional newscaster is inadvertently flipping off all her viewers. As you probably guessed, shortly after this incident she was no longer reporting the news for Channel 7.

Don't let this happen to you. You must remain physically and mentally in the game even as the other person is shutting down their end of the interview. After your five minutes of thoughtful recollection, silently turn off your microphone, your camera, your computer, and your lighting. Remain in a professional mode as you do this and reconfirm that everything is powered off before you get up from your seat. You have worked very hard to successfully complete this interview, so make sure your hard work pays off.

Moral of the Story	*Don't blow your victory on unsportsmanlike behavior after the ninth inning. Remain professional, stay on your game, and give yourself the best chance for success.*

INDEX

A

"action position," 139
action story, frame your narrative as an, 143-146
action words, 146
A-game, be on your, 103, 161
audio, test your, 51
audio equipment,
   high quality, 35
   upgrade your, 35

B

background,
   best colors for a, 46, 47, 48, 121-122
   coordinating your outfit with your, 122
   how to create a, 45-49
   test your, 51
   using a professional, 46
   using a stand for your, 47-48
   using fabric to create, 48
   using poster board to create, 46-47
   using seamless paper to create, 46
   worst colors for your, 46, 122
backup plan, have a, 71-72
bandwith, increase your, 65

barriers, remove all, 141-142
battery,
   charge your laptop, 67-68
   test out your, 67
blooper,
   get back on track after a, 191
   way to use a, 192
bloopers, 191-193
   benefit from your, 192
Blue Snowball USB microphone, 35-36, 65
   shockmount for your, 36

C

camera
   angle, the best, 63-64
   lens, clean your, 57-58
camera,
   built-in laptop, 32
   choosing a, 31-34
   correct positioning of your, 59, 63-64
   get comfortable in front of the, 97-98, 175
   make love to the, 175-177
   transfer emotion through the, 175
   using a level to level your, 59-60
   using a tripod to position the, 59

About the Author

Paul Bailo is CEO and founder of Phone Interview Pro. He holds a bachelor's degree in science from St. John's University, a master's in clinical social work from Fordham University, and a master's in business administration from Wagner College. He is currently completing his doctorate at the International School of Management in Paris, France.

He has been an adjunct professor at Sacred Heart University in Fairfield, Connecticut, for the past 10 years. He has more than 15 years of experience working for Fortune 500 companies and organizations such as Citibank, the Federal Reserve Bank of New York, GE Money, and American Express, all of which he credits for giving him the necessary experience to write this book. His previous book with Career Press, *The Essential Phone Interview Handbook*, has been published in several languages and countries, and has helped countless people hone their phone interview skills.

Paul's ultimate goal is to help people get back to work. In these uncertain economic times, he believes that every person in America who wants to work should work, and, ideally, should have multiple options available. He also believes that it's more important than ever that candidates present themselves in the best, most attractive light possible. He's done his research by interviewing countless candidates, building a test line for microphones and cameras, building mock studios, and talking to professionals in various industries.

Now he wants to share what he's learned to help people with their digital job interviews. In doing this, he reaches his own goal of helping as many people as possible.

Paul grew up in Queens, New York, and now lives in Trumbull, Connecticut, with his wife and two children.

If you have any comments or questions about the book, feel free to e-mail the author at *executive@phoneinterviewpro.com*.

What Is Phone Interview Pro?

Phone Interview Pro began as a company designed to help job candidates ace their phone interviews. It is a three-part company that offers a mock phone interview with a high-level executive, a copy of *The Official Phone Interview Handbook*, and an online educational program. This company has grown rapidly since its birth, becoming a part of outsourcing agencies and educational institutions. With this book it has expanded to the next logical chapter: the digital interview.

Paul is available for speaking events. You can contact him at *executive@phoneinterviewpro.com*.